CAMBRIDGE PRIMARY
Science

Learner's Book

6

Fiona Baxter, Liz Dilley and Jon Board

CAMBRIDGE
UNIVERSITY PRESS

CAMBRIDGE
UNIVERSITY PRESS

University Printing House, Cambridge CB2 8BS, United Kingdom

One Liberty Plaza, 20th Floor, New York, NY 10006, USA

477 Williamstown Road, Port Melbourne, VIC 3207, Australia

314–321, 3rd Floor, Plot 3, Splendor Forum, Jasola District Centre, New Delhi – 110025, India

79 Anson Road, #06–04/06, Singapore 079906

Cambridge University Press is part of the University of Cambridge.

It furthers the University's mission by disseminating knowledge in the pursuit of education, learning and research at the highest international levels of excellence.

www.cambridge.org
Information on this title: www.cambridge.org/9781107699809

First published 2014

20 19 18 17

Printed in Malaysia by Vivar Printing

A catalogue record for this publication is available from the British Library

ISBN 978-1-107-69980-9 Paperback

Cover artwork: Bill Bolton

....

The publisher is grateful to the experienced teachers Mansoora Shoaib Shah, Lahore Grammar School, 55 Main, Gulberg, Lahore and Lynne Ransford for their careful reviewing of the content.

Introduction to teachers

The *Cambridge Primary Science* series has been developed to match the Cambridge International Examinations Primary Science curriculum framework. It is a fun, flexible and easy-to-use course that gives both learners and teachers the support they need. In keeping with the aims of the curriculum itself, it encourages learners to be actively engaged with the content, and develop enquiry skills as well as subject knowledge.

This Learner's Book for Stage 6 covers all the content from Stage 6 of the curriculum framework. The topics are covered in the order in which they are presented in the curriculum for easy navigation, but can be taught in any order that is appropriate to you.

Throughout the book you will find ideas for practical activities, which will help learners to develop their Scientific Enquiry skills as well as introduce them to the thrill of scientific discovery.

The 'Talk about it!' question in each topic can be used as a starting point for classroom discussion, encouraging learners to use the scientific vocabulary and develop their understanding.

'Check your progress' questions at the end of each unit can be used to assess learners' understanding. Learners who will be taking the Cambridge Primary Progression Test for Stage 6 will find these questions useful preparation.

We strongly advise you to use the Teacher's Resource for Stage 6, ISBN 978-1-107-66202-5, alongside this book. This resource contains extensive guidance on all the topics, ideas for classroom activities, and guidance notes on all the activities presented in this Learners' Book. You will also find a large collection of worksheets, and answers to all the questions from the Stage 6 products.

Also available is the Activity Book for Stage 6, ISBN 978-1-107-64375-8. This book offers a variety of exercises to help learners consolidate understanding, practise vocabulary, apply knowledge to new situations and develop enquiry skills. Learners can complete the exercises in class or be given them as homework.

We hope you enjoy using this series.

With best wishes,
the Cambridge Primary Science team.

Contents

1 Humans and animals

1.1 Body organs

You know what the outside of your body looks like. But what's inside your body? Think of as many inside parts as you can.

The parts inside your body are called **organs**. The body organs do different jobs to keep you alive and healthy.

Different organs work together to form **organ systems**.

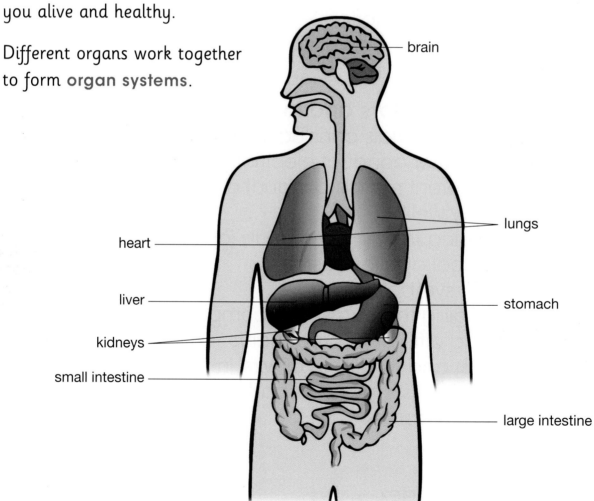

The liver is an example of a body organ. We cannot live without a liver. Two of its main functions are to store energy and to break down harmful substances in the body.

Identifying the position of body organs

Lie down on the newspaper and ask your
partner to draw the outline of your body.
Don't draw around the arms and legs.
Draw outlines of these body organs on the white paper:

- brain
- heart
- stomach
- lungs
- kidneys
- intestines.

Make sure each organ is the right size for the body outline you have drawn.
Label and colour each organ.
Cut out the organs and stick them in the right place on the body.

> **You will need:**
> a newspaper · white paper ·
> colouring pens · crayons ·
> glue · scissors

Questions

1 Which organ is found in the in head?

2 Which organs are found in the chest?

3 Which organs are found in pairs?

4 Which organs are found in the chest?

5 What do you think is the function of each body organ?

Some animals, like the jellyfish, do not have proper body organs. They have more simple parts that carry out their body functions.

What you have learnt

- The parts inside your body are called organs.
- The major body organs are the heart, stomach and intestines, lungs, kidneys and brain.

Talk about it!

How are the body organs protected?

1.2 The heart

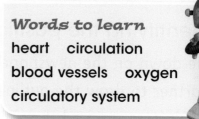

Put your hand on your chest. Can you feel your **heart** beating? Why does your heart beat?

Make a fist with your hand. That's how big your heart is. Your heart is found inside your chest, slightly to the left. It is protected by the ribs.

Your heart is a special muscle. Its job is to pump blood through your body. This process is called **circulation**. Every time the heart muscle squeezes to pump blood, you can feel a heartbeat. It takes less than a minute to pump blood to every part of your body. The heart does this all the time and never stops.

The heart has two sides. The left side (red in the diagram) pumps blood that contains **oxygen** all around the body. The right side (blue in the diagram) pumps blood without oxygen to the lungs only.

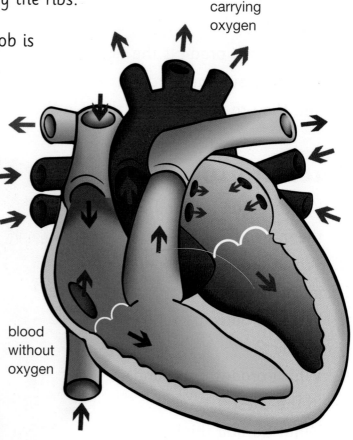

blood carrying oxygen

blood without oxygen

Why must the heart pump blood around the body?

Blood is a red liquid that flows around the body in **blood vessels**. Look at the inside of your wrist. Sometimes you can see the blood vessels through your skin.

Blood vessels run from the heart to the lungs, around the body and back to the heart.

The blood carries food and oxygen to all parts of the body. It also picks up waste products from the body and carries them to organs which can get rid of them. The kidneys and lungs are two of these organs.

The heart, blood vessels and blood form the **circulatory system**.

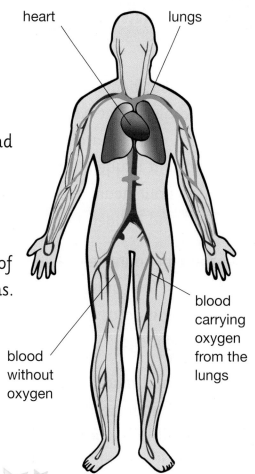

heart   lungs

blood carrying oxygen from the lungs

blood without oxygen

Questions

1 **a** What does the heart do?
   b Why does it do this?
2 What is a heartbeat?
3 Why does the heart pump blood to the lungs before it pumps blood to the rest of the body?

Challenge

What is a heart attack and how is it caused?

What you have learnt

- The left side of the heart pumps blood that contains oxygen to the rest of the body.
- The right side pumps blood without oxygen to the lungs.
- The blood carries food and oxygen to all parts of the body and carries away waste products from the different parts of the body.

Talk about it!

How can you tell that your heart is beating without putting a hand on your chest?

1.3 Heartbeat and pulse

Your heat beats about 90 times a minute. When you are grown up it will beat about 70 times a minute. When you run around, your body needs a lot more food and oxygen. The more active you are, the more often your heart needs to beat to supply enough food and oxygen from the blood.

You can count your heartbeats by feeling your **pulse**. Your pulse is caused by the **pressure** of the blood as the heart pumps it to the rest of the body.

Two good places to find your pulse are on the side of your neck and the inside of your wrist. You will know you've found your pulse when you feel a small beat under your skin. Each beat is caused by the squeezing of your heart muscle.

Exercise makes your heart beat faster.

Activity 1.3

Measuring your pulse

You will need:
a watch with a second hand

Find your pulse on your wrist or neck. Do not use your thumb to take your pulse – it has a pulse of its own. Count how many beats you feel in one minute. Repeat this three times. Record the results in a table. Is the number of beats the same each time? Compare your measurements with others in your class.
Measure your pulse rate at other times during the day, such as after lunch break and just before you go to bed. What trends can you identify?

Questions

1. What is the difference between heartbeat and pulse?
2. Did everyone in your group have the same pulse rate?
3. a Is your pulse rate always the same?
   b Why do you think this is?
   c How can you work out what your actual pulse rate is?
4. Suggest any factors you think make your pulse rate change.

The elephant has a very low pulse rate of 30 beats per minute.
The mouse has very high pulse rate of 500 beats per minute.

What you have learnt

- You can count your heartbeats by feeling your pulse.
- Your pulse feels like a small beat under the skin.
- Your pulse rate increases when you exercise.

Talk about it!
Why is it dangerous to have a very low pulse rate?

1.4 The lungs and breathing

We use our **lungs** for **breathing**. We need to breathe to stay alive. We breathe in and breathe out.

The lungs are found in the chest. They are protected by the ribs. The lungs are like stretchy sponges that fill up with air.

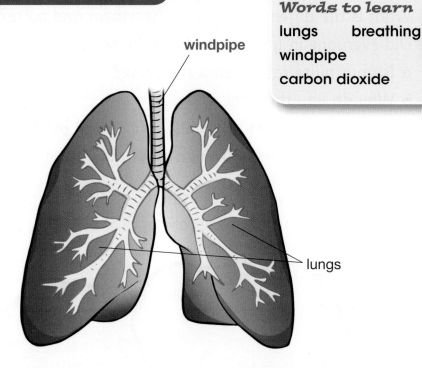

windpipe

lungs

Activity 1.4

Investigating breathing

You will need:
a balloon

Put your hands on your ribcage.
Breathe in. What do you feel?
Now breathe out. What do you feel?
Breathe in again. Hold the balloon to your mouth and breathe out. What happens to the balloon?
What does this show you?

Questions

1   When you breathe in, does your chest get bigger or smaller?
    Why do you think this is so?

2   When you breathe out, does your chest get bigger or smaller?
    Why do you think this is so?

3   Explain how we are able to blow up a balloon.

4   Why do you think we breathe faster when we exercise?

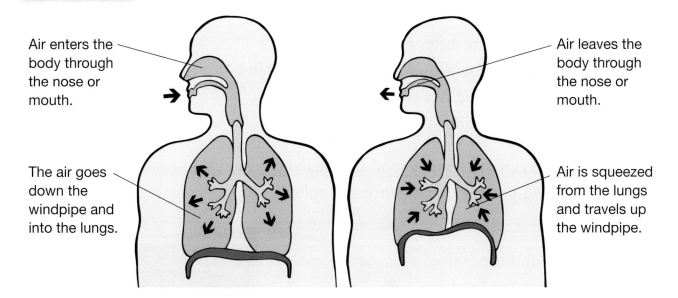

Air enters the body through the nose or mouth.

The air goes down the windpipe and into the lungs.

Air leaves the body through the nose or mouth.

Air is squeezed from the lungs and travels up the windpipe.

When we breathe in, oxygen from the air moves into the blood vessels in the lungs. Blood carries the oxygen to the heart and then to the other parts of the body. We need oxygen to live.

As your body uses up oxygen, it makes **carbon dioxide**. Carbon dioxide is a waste gas that the body must get rid of. The blood carries the carbon dioxide back to the lungs. We get rid of carbon dioxide in the air we breathe out.

Talk about it!
How do divers breathe underwater?

What you have learnt
- We use our lungs for breathing.
- Our lungs get bigger and fill with air when we breathe in.
- Our lungs get smaller and push out air when we breathe out.
- We breathe in oxygen from the air.
- We breathe out carbon dioxide.

1.5 The digestive system

Your body needs food to help it grow. Food also gives you energy. But your body cannot use the food you eat just as it is. Food has to be changed so that it can be used by the body.

The **digestive system** changes food by breaking it down into tiny particles. This process is called **digestion**.

The **stomach** and the **intestines** digest the food. They are the main organs of the digestive system. Digested food particles pass from the intestine into the blood and are carried to all parts of the body.

The food we eat must be digested so that the body can use it.

Questions

1   Why do we need food?
2   Why must food be digested?
3   How does the stomach help digestion?
4   What happens to food in the intestines?
5   How does the digested food reach all parts of the body?

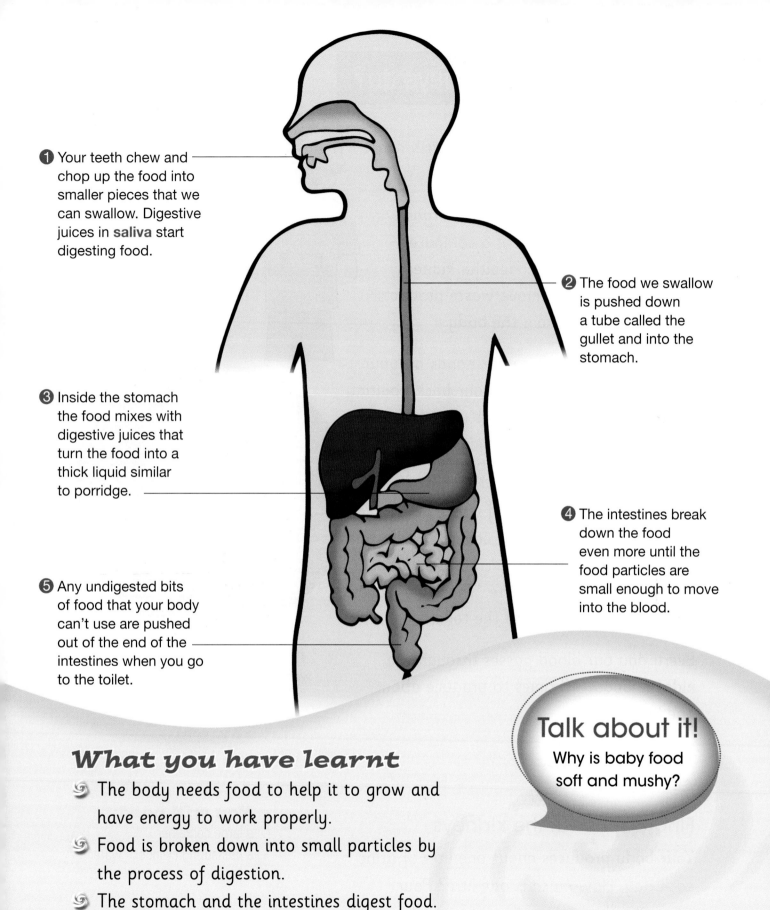

1 Your teeth chew and chop up the food into smaller pieces that we can swallow. Digestive juices in **saliva** start digesting food.

2 The food we swallow is pushed down a tube called the gullet and into the stomach.

3 Inside the stomach the food mixes with digestive juices that turn the food into a thick liquid similar to porridge.

4 The intestines break down the food even more until the food particles are small enough to move into the blood.

5 Any undigested bits of food that your body can't use are pushed out of the end of the intestines when you go to the toilet.

What you have learnt

- The body needs food to help it to grow and have energy to work properly.
- Food is broken down into small particles by the process of digestion.
- The stomach and the intestines digest food.
- Digested food is carried in the blood to all parts of the body.

Talk about it!

Why is baby food soft and mushy?

1.6 What do the kidneys do?

The **kidneys** are found below the rib cage at the back of the body.

They are a pair of bean-shaped organs, in an adult about the size of a computer mouse. Healthy adult. Healthy kidneys filter the blood to remove waste products and excess water from the body.

Find your kidneys. Put your hands on your hips with your thumbs on your back pointing backwards. Slide your hands up until you can feel your ribs. Your kidneys are just under your thumbs.

The process of removing of waste products from the body is called **excretion**. The kidneys excrete a liquid waste product called **urine**. The urine leaves our body when we go to the toilet.

Every day our blood passes through the kidneys about 40 times to produce about one litre of urine.

Drink six to eight glasses of water each day to keep your kidneys healthy.

Activity 1.6

Find out about the kidneys

Your body produces about one litre of urine each day. How much is one litre? Pour what you think is one litre of water into the container. How can you check?

You will need:
a large container
a measuring cylinder • water

When the kidneys don't work

If one kidney stops working because of **disease**, doctors can remove it. Your body can still work well with one healthy kidney.

Some people don't have healthy kidneys and their kidneys stop working. They need to go on a machine that acts like a kidney to filter and clean the blood. This is called **dialysis** (we say di-al-i-siss).

Sometimes people have a kidney transplant. This means that they get a kidney from another person, often someone in their family.

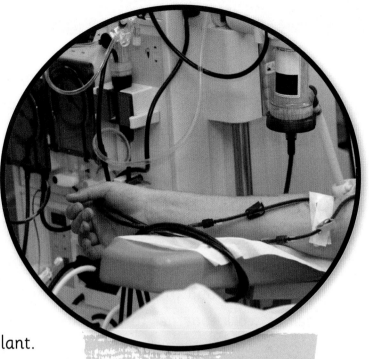

Dialysis machines are very expensive and dialysis takes several hours a day for three days a week.

Questions

1 Where are your kidneys found in the body?

2 What size are the kidneys?

3 **a** What is the name of the main process carried out by the kidneys?

   b Explain how the kidneys carry out this process.

4 Name **three** things doctors can do if your kidneys don't work.

What you have learnt

- The kidneys are pair of organs found at the back of the body, below the ribs.
- The main function of the kidneys is to remove waste from the body as urine. This is called excretion.

Talk about it!

Why do you produce less urine in hot weather than in cold weather?

1.7 What does the brain do?

How do you remember your way home from school?
Why do you breathe without thinking about it?
How do you know when you are hungry or thirsty?
Where do dreams come from?

The brain is a soft, grey, wrinkly organ inside your skull. It does all your learning and thinking and also controls all your muscles and senses.

The brain is connected to all parts of the body by nerves. Nerves send messages to and from the brain very quickly all the time. The brain and nerves work together to form the nervous system.

Different parts of the brain have different jobs.

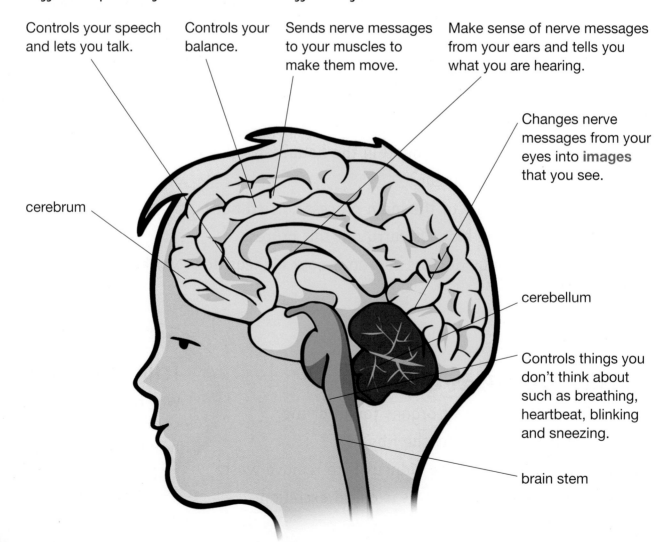

Controls your speech and lets you talk.

Controls your balance.

Sends nerve messages to your muscles to make them move.

Make sense of nerve messages from your ears and tells you what you are hearing.

Changes nerve messages from your eyes into images that you see.

cerebrum

cerebellum

Controls things you don't think about such as breathing, heartbeat, blinking and sneezing.

brain stem

What happens if your brain is damaged?

When the brain is damaged it is serious because the brain controls everything we do. Some body organs can repair themselves, others can't. The brain usually cannot repair itself.

Some things that affect the brain are germs that cause infections, growths on the brain called tumours, lack of oxygen and head injuries.

Questions

1 a How is the brain protected?

   b Why is it important to protect the brain?

2 a How does the brain send messages to, and receive messages from, other parts of the body?

   b Why is it important that these messages travel very quickly? Think about this situation: you are crossing the road when suddenly you see a car speeding towards you.

3 Explain how your brain allows you to make a phone call to a friend.

Challenge

What is concussion?

Dreams are the thoughts, images and sounds formed by our brains while we are asleep. Dreams can be about anything and often don't make any sense when we remember them. We have several dreams every night but we don't remember most of them.

What you have learnt

- The brain is protected by the skull.
- The brain controls everything – our body movements, senses, speech, heartbeat and breathing.
- Brain injuries are serious because the brain controls everything and cannot repair itself.

Talk about it!

Does your brain still work when you are asleep? How do we know this?

1 Match each organ in column A with its main function in column B.

A	B
heart	excretion
stomach and intestines	breathing
lungs	control
kidneys	digestion
brain	circulation

2 State whether each of the following statements is true or false. Correct the false statements.

a The heart pumps air around the body.

b Your heart beats faster when you exercise.

c Your pulse rate tells you how fast you are exercising.

d Blood moves around the body in special tubes called blood vessels.

e The blood picks up carbon dioxide in the lungs.

3 Use the words in the box to complete the sentences about digestion.

> mouth   stomach   intestines   gullet

a Food is pushed down the _____ into the stomach.

b In the _____ , the food is broken down into very small particles.

c The food is mixed with digestive juices in the _____ .

d Undigested food is pushed out of the body through the end of the _____ .

e The food is chewed in the _____ .

4 The sentences in **3** are in the wrong order. Sort them into the correct order of the stages of digestion.

5

a Name the organs shown in the pictures.

b Which organ removes wastes and excess water from the body?

c What is the waste from this organ called?

d Which organ allows us to think, talk and move?

e How does B make sure that A does its job?

f How does playing a game of soccer affect A's function?

g How is A protected from damage?

h How is B protected from damage?

A

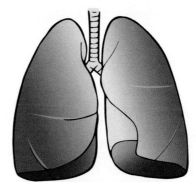

B

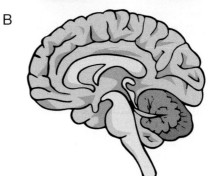

C

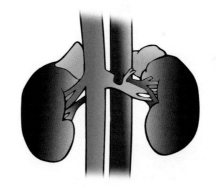

6

a Name the waste gas that we breathe out of the lungs.

b Name the gas we breathe into the lungs.

2 Living things in the environment

2.1 Food chains in a local habitat

Lindiwe lives in Zambia. She is proud of her vegetable garden. She grows maize, spinach and pumpkins. Although vegetables grow fast in the warm sun, it is the dry season so Lindiwe must water her garden every day.

The vegetable garden is the home or habitat of many plants and animals. There is a **feeding relationship** between some plants and animals. For example, caterpillars eat spinach leaves and stalk borers make holes in the maize stalks. Other animals help to fight these **pests**. Some birds eat caterpillars and lizards eat stalk borers.

The leaf is food for the caterpillar.

Food chains

We can **depict** a feeding relationship using a **food chain**. A food chain describes the feeding relationship between a plant and an animal. One food chain is:

spinach → caterpillar

The arrow means 'is eaten by'. So this food chain tells us that spinach is eaten by the caterpillar.

Look at food chains 1 and 2, opposite. Write each one in words with an arrow.

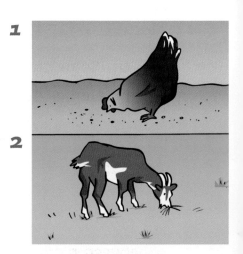

Activity 2.1

Describe a habitat in your area

Visit a local habitat such as a garden.
Identify the species of plants and
animals.

List all the plants and animals you
can see.

Look under leaves on bushes and under
dead leaves on the ground to find
insects. Look in the sky and in
the trees for birds.

Observe feeding relationships between
plants and animals.

Discuss other ways that plants and
animals depend on each other in
your habitat.

Questions

1 Name **three** plants and **three** animals in your habitat.
2 Draw **three** food chains to represent feeding relationships that you observed.
3 How else do plants and animals depend on each other in your habitat?
4 Draw **two** food chains involving a plant and an animal in Lindiwe's garden.

What you have learnt

🌀 A habitat is a home in the environment for
plants and animals.

🌀 Food chains describe the feeding relationship
between plants and animals.

> **Talk about it!**
> What would animals
> and humans eat if we
> had no plants?

2.2 Food chains begin with plants

Plants

Everything that we, and all animals do, such as moving, breathing, eating and sleeping, needs **energy**. We get energy from food. All our food comes from plants. We either eat plants or we eat animals which have eaten plants. Look back to the food chains in Topic 2.1. Each began with a plant.

Plants are **unique** because they produce their own food. For this reason we call a plant a **producer**. Animals and humans cannot make their own food. They eat or consume plants so an animals is called a **consumer**.

Look again at the feeding relationships in these two food chains.

Plants are essential to life on Earth.

1
2

In food chain 1, the corn is the producer and the chicken is the consumer.

Identify the producer and consumer in food chain 2.

If a boy eats the chicken in 1, he is also a consumer. So now the food chain is:

corn → chicken → human

Questions

1 Rearrange the living things in each feeding relationship to make food chains:
   a spinach bird caterpillar
   b human grass sheep

How do plants make food?

Plants make food in their leaves from sunlight, water and carbon dioxide. A plant must have all three of these **factors**. If a plant gets sunlight and carbon dioxide, but not enough water, it will wither. In this unhealthy state it will not make food.

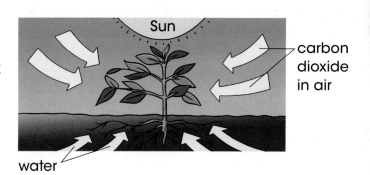

The plant takes in energy from the Sun and uses it to change water and carbon dioxide into sugar and oxygen. It stores the sugar. The oxygen is a waste product, so the plant sends it back to the air.

When an animal eats a plant it gets energy from the sugar stored in the plant.

Plants also take in nutrients such as iron and magnesium. These are dissolved in water in the soil. The plant takes in the water and nutrients through its roots.

Activity 2.2

Investigating what plants need to survive and make food

Plan two investigations to show (1) that plants need water, and (2) that plants need sunlight.

Before you begin, predict what will happen to your plants.

You will need:
four pots with healthy seedlings

Questions

1 Identify the factor relevant in each investigation.
2 What did you predict in each investigation?
3 What evidence did you find to support your predictions? Suggest explanations for your predictions based on what you know already.

What you have learnt

🌀 Plants are producers because they make their own food.
🌀 Animals are consumers because they eat plants.

Talk about it!
What happens to all the oxygen that plants put back into the air?

2.3 Consumers in food chains

Consumers

Some animals eat mainly plants. Some animals eat other animals. An animal that eats other animals is called a **predator**. The animals that it kills and eats are its **prey**. Look at these examples.

The owl is a predator and his prey is the mouse.

A frog is a predator because it eats insects. The frog has to be quick – it shoots out its sticky tongue to catch its prey.

Snakes are predators. Some kill their prey with venom (poison) but this snake is swallowing its prey (an egg) whole.

Sometimes there is more than one predator in a food chain.

The grasshopper eats the plant. Then the grasshopper becomes the prey for the lizard, which is the predator. Then the lizard becomes the prey of the hawk, which is another predator.

Questions

1 Think back to your local habitat. Name **two** predators. What is the prey for each predator?

2 Look at the animals in the picture. There are five predators and their prey. Match each predator with its prey.

3 Draw a food chain to depict one of the predator and prey pairs. Start with a producer.

4 Identify the pattern in the food chains you have described.

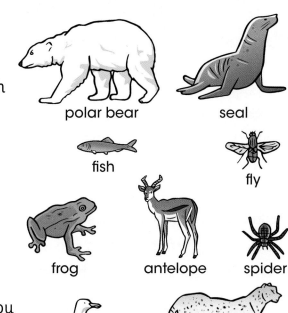

polar bear   seal

fish

fly

frog   antelope   spider

seagull   cheetah

Challenge

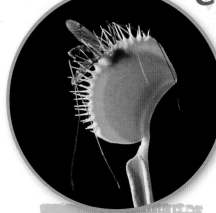

A Venus fly trap catching a fly.

The Venus flytrap grows in soils which have few nutrients. It can make sugar from sunlight, like other plants. But it also traps flies and dissolves them. It uses nutrients from the fly's body. Why is it so useful for the fly trap to trap flies? Can you find out the names of **two** more predator plants?

What you have learnt

- Predators are consumers that eat other animals.
- Animals eaten by predators are called their prey.

Talk about it!

Are there any animals that never become prey for another animal?

2.4 Food chains in different habitats

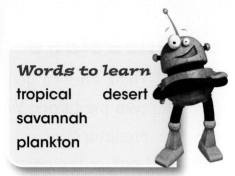

Words to learn
tropical   desert
savannah
plankton

Different habitats

There are many habitats on the Earth. This is because there are many climates which result in different plants. In hot wet climates there are **tropical** forests. In dry climates only a few **desert** plants grow. Different plants attract different animals. So we find different food chains according to the habitat.

Food chains in a savannah habitat

The **savannah** covers a large part of Africa. It is hot all year and the rain comes mainly in summer. Grass and scattered trees grow there. Some animals eat the grass and trees. Others are predators.

This is a food chain in a savannah habitat. Discuss what is happening in the food chain. Which are the producers? Which are the consumers? Which consumers are predators and which are prey? What does each animal eat?

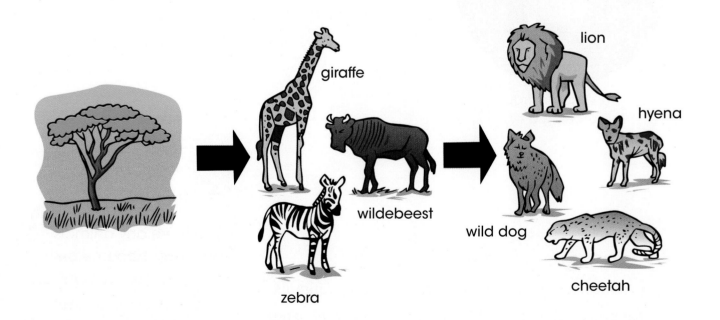

Food chains in an ocean habitat

Almost three quarters of the Earth's surface is ocean, so ocean habitats are very important.
There are many types of seaweed. Most plants and animals are so small you can't see them with the naked eye. These are called **plankton**. Some sea animals only eat plankton. Others are predators.

Discuss what you can see in the picture of a food chain in the ocean. Which are the producers, predators and prey? Who is eating who?

The basking shark can reach a length of 8 m but it eats only plankton.

Questions

1   Compare the producers in the savannah and ocean habitats.

2   In the savannah habitat:
    a Name **three** animals that only eat plants. Which plants do they eat?
    b Draw **two** food chains containing predator and prey relationships.

3   In the ocean habitat:
    a Draw **two** food chains containing one predator and its prey.
    b Draw **two** food chains containing two predators and their prey.

What you have learnt

🌀 Different habitats contain different plants and animals. This leads to different food chains.

Talk about it!
What would happen if all predators in the savannah habitat suddenly died?

2.5 Deforestation

Words to learn

deforestation
negative
environment
greenhouse gases
global warming
conserve

Tropical rainforests are cut down at the rate of one football field every second! **Deforestation** happens when we destroy forests by cutting down trees. Why does this happen? The main reasons are:

- to collect wood to make furniture
- to collect wood to burn as a fuel
- to clear land for farming
- to clear land for cities
- to clear land for mining.

Deforestation has **negative** effects on the **environment**. When trees are cut down in the rainforest, it can take 100 years for new trees to become fully grown. Without trees, there are no rotting leaves to make compost. This makes the soil poor. Grasses grow, but not trees. Plants and animals in the forest will disappear.

Cattle grazing on land that used to be covered with forest.

Trees take carbon dioxide from the air to make food. So forests remove carbon dioxide and help to reduce **global warming**. Also, trees give out oxygen which humans and animals need to survive.

Why are forests so important?

Habitats
In a patch of rainforest 6 km square, there can be 1500 kinds of plant, 400 kinds of bird, 150 kinds of butterfly and 100 kinds of reptile.

Medicines
People who live in the forests have found many plants that cure human diseases. A lot of modern drugs were originally made from forest plants.

Removing carbon dioxide and giving us oxygen
The Earth is becoming hotter because humans are putting more gases like carbon dioxide into the air. These are called greenhouse gases because they trap the heat like a greenhouse does. The process where the Earth is getting warmer is called global warming.

Activity 2.5

Plant a tree

You can help remove carbon dioxide from the air by planting a tree. Go to a plant nursery or a friend with a garden and ask them to donate a seedling. What kind of tree would you like? How about a shade tree? Would you like a fruit tree?

Ask the person how and where to plant your tree and how often you must water it.

Questions

1   Identify **three** negative factors that result from deforestation.
2   Compare the soil in a forest area before and after deforestation.
3   Explain why buying second-hand wooden furniture is a good way to conserve forests.
4   Predict what would happen to the carbon dioxide and oxygen in the air if all forests were destroyed.

What you have learnt

- Deforestation happens when people destroy forests by cutting down trees.
- Deforestation has a negative effect on the environment.

Talk about it!
Why do you think that forests are called the 'Lungs of the Earth'?

2.6 Air pollution

Words to learn
pollution
pollutants
bronchitis
asthma

Our **atmosphere** consists mainly of two gases: nitrogen and oxygen. There are smaller amounts of carbon dioxide and water vapour. None of these gases are harmful. But people pollute our atmosphere with particles of other gases.

Cars, motorcycles, buses and trucks give off carbon monoxide in exhaust fumes.

Carbon monoxide is poisonous. New cars are less polluting than older ones because they are fitted with a device that changes the exhaust gases into carbon dioxide.

We burn coal and oil to give us energy. Wind power, solar power and water power do not cause **pollution**, but for many countries they are more expensive than coal or oil.

Coal and oil burnt in factories and power stations give off the gases sulfur dioxide and nitrogen oxide.

Sometimes **pollutants** are blown away by the wind. But often dirty air lies over cities. Pollution has a negative effect on plants and animals. People in polluted areas often get **bronchitis** and **asthma**.

Measure dirt particles in the air

Mark an area of 4 × 1 cm with a marker pen on one side of each slide. Number the slides 1 to 5. Cover the other side of each slide with a thin layer of petroleum jelly.

Tape the slides to five different sites. The petroleum jelly must face outwards. Choose sites where your slides will not be disturbed. Leave these slides for one week. Then carefully put the slides in a box and bring them to school. Do not to touch the petroleum jelly. Predict which slide is going to have the most pollution. Give reasons. Examine each slide with a hand lens. Can you see particles of dirt? Count the number of particles in each marked area.

Record your results on a table. Draw a bar chart of your results.

> **You will need:**
> five glass slides
> petroleum jelly • a marker pen
> tape • a hand lens

Make sure the petroleum jelly is facing out.

Questions

1 Compare your results with other groups. Which site is most polluted? Can you explain why?
2 Identify the pattern in your results. Did any sites not fit the pattern that you expected?
3 Did the evidence you collected support your predictions?
4 Work in a group to produce an information leaflet on another type of pollution. You could choose water or land pollution. Present your information to the class.

What you have learnt

- Air pollution is caused by exhaust fumes and gases from coal and oil that is burnt in factories and power stations.
- It has negative effects on the environment and peoples' health.

Talk about it!
What causes air pollution in your country?

2.7 Acid rain

All around the world, trees are dying. This is happening because of a kind of pollution called **acid rain**.

When coal, oil and natural gas are burnt, they give off sulfur dioxide and nitrogen oxides. These gases dissolve in rainwater to form sulfuric acid and nitric acid. This makes the rain into acid rain. It can be as acidic as lemon juice.

The picture shows how acid rain forms. The acid rain drains into lakes and makes the water in them acidic.

Acid rain 'eats away' at stone and damages buildings.

Activity 2.7

Observe the effect of acid rain

Water one seedling with tap water.
Water the other with lemon juice.
Predict what will happen using what you know about acid rain.
Observe what happens over the next few days.

You will need:
two healthy seedlings growing in soil • tap water
lemon juice

Questions

1 Compare the two plants after five days.
  What has happened to:
  a the leaves
  b the stems?

2 Do these results support your predictions? How?

3 Use what you have learnt about acid rain to explain why these changes happened.

4 Research how acid rain can damage buildings.

How does acid rain affect the environment?

Soil contains nutrients that keep plants healthy. Plants take in nutrients through their roots. But acid rain washes nutrients out of the soil. The lack of nutrients weakens plants. They grow slowly and their leaves fall off. Plants need leaves to make food. With fewer leaves, plants make less food.

Even large trees are damaged by acid rain. Pest attack can kill them because they are so weak and their branches die back. Eventually the trees die.

Acid rain damages pine needles at the end of the branches.

All the leaves have fallen due to acid rain.

The number of frogs is falling worldwide. Acid rain damages frogspawn and kills insects that frogs eat.

What you have learnt

- Acid rain is caused by sulfur dioxide dissolving in rainwater to form an acid.
- Acid rain damages plants, animals living in water and stone buildings.

Talk about it!
How could you demonstrate that acid rain damages stonework?

2.8 Recycling

Waste disposal is a problem. How do we get rid of the mountains of rubbish we all throw away? Most of it is taken to **landfill** sites like the one in the picture. Landfill sites are huge piles of rubbish near towns that are later covered with soil. If we can **reduce** the amount of our rubbish, we will be helping the environment.

Recycling is when something is not thrown away but processed into something that can be used again. Reducing and recycling is something everyone can do at home, at school and at work. Next time you are going to put something in the bin, stop and think. Could it be recycled?

Landfill sites take up valuable land which could be used for other things.

This jar has been reused to collect tadpoles.

Thabiso makes toy chickens like this one out of plastic bags. He has recycled the bags.

Save the environment by recycling

Reusing and recycling are **positive** ways you can care for the environment by saving natural materials.

Millions of trees are cut down to make wood pulp for paper. If you recycle paper, fewer trees are cut down.

Use glass containers again or take them to be recycled. Glass can be melted down and reshaped to make new containers. It never becomes weaker.

Drink cans are made from aluminium which can be recycled. It takes a lot of electricity to get aluminium from the rock it is found in. Recycling aluminium uses much less energy.

Many types of plastic never rot away. Recycling plastic is expensive. Use things again instead of throwing them away. Reduce the plastic you use. If possible, don't buy fruit in plastic trays.

Don't throw away all your kitchen and garden waste. You can recycle it by making **compost**. This will be good for the soil and your plants will grow better.

Activity 2.8

Make compost

Collect vegetable peelings, fruit, egg shells.
Collect grass cuttings, leaves and weeds.
Put the waste into the bag.
Add some water but do not make it too wet.
Leave the compost in a warm place for a few weeks. When the compost is dark and mushy, it is ready. Spread it on the soil around your plants.

You will need:
a large plastic bag
food scraps · garden waste

Questions

1 Suggest ways that you can use less paper.
2 Suggest ways you can reuse plastic containers.
3 Suggest how compost could help your plants.
4 Encourage people to recycle. Make a poster to put in a local hall.

Challenge

Go to the supermarket. List products in packaging that can be recycled.

What you have learnt

- Recycling is when something is not thrown away but processed into something that can be used again.
- Re-using and recycling helps to care for our environment.

Talk about it!
How can you and your family re-use and recycle at home?

2.9 Take care of your environment

Words to learn

resource

audit

Conserve our water and energy

Everyone can care for our environment by using less water and energy. This helps to conserve each **resource**.

You can conserve (use less) water quite easily. Here are some ideas.

- Have a shower instead of a bath.
- Never leave a tap dripping.
- Collect rainwater in a tank and use it for washing.
- Discuss other ways you can use less water.

You can conserve (use less) energy quite easily. Here are some ideas.

- Switch off electricity when you are not using it.
- Use energy-efficient bulbs.
- Walk or ride a bike rather than using a car or bus.
- Use solar panels to heat your water. They are much cheaper and cleaner than using an electric heater.
- Discuss other ways you can reduce energy consumption.

Litter

Litter pollutes our environment. It looks horrible, it is dirty and it smells. It harms animals who eat it, thinking that it is food.

Turtles eat plastic bags because they mistake them for jellyfish. The plastic stays in their stomachs and they die.

Activity 2.9

Do a litter clean-up and a litter audit

You can **audit** litter by counting how many cans, bottles, papers and other things people throw away. This will help you to see how much rubbish can be recycled.

Work in pairs to collect the litter, record it and put the litter into the bag.

Leave the bag at a collection point for it to be taken away.

Predict what will be the most common type of litter.

Make a list of all the kinds of litter you found.

Then add up how many items of each kind you collected.

Make a table to record your results.

Present your results in a bar chart.

> **You will need:**
> large dustbin bag
> notepad and pencil
> rubber gloves

Safety Wear rubber gloves when picking up rubbish and be careful of broken glass.

Questions

1 Did the evidence you collected in your audit support your predictions?

2 Compare the patterns in the results from everyone in the class. Do any audits not fit the pattern? Can you explain this?

3 Start an anti-litter campaign. Make posters to put up around your school.

What you have learnt

- We can care for the environment by conserving water and energy.
- We can stop littering to help to care for the environment.

Talk about it!
What can you do in your community to stop littering?

2 Check your progress

1 Write a list of the words in Column A. Choose the correct meaning for each word from column B. Write the correct meaning beside each word.

Column A	Column B
recycle	a place where plant and animals live together
habitat	a feeding relationship between plants and animals
nutrient	to reprocess something so that it can be used again
global warming	another name for a food
food chain	the worldwide increase in temperature

2 Look at the picture below.

Identify the following in the picture:

    a the source of energy

    b two producers

    c four consumers

    d a predator and its prey

3 In the picture, what would happen if:

    a all the insects disappeared?

    b the Sun stopped shining forever?

4 Write these food chains so that the living things are in the correct order.

    a Lion → grass → wildebeest

    b Plankton → seagull → fish

    c Beetle → lizard → seeds → hawk

    d Shark → plankton → small fish → seal

5 Choose **three** predators and their prey from the living things in **4**.

6 Explain how:

    a Deforestation helps to cause global warming.

    b Frogs can be killed by acid rain.

7 Describe how each of these things can be recycled or re-used:

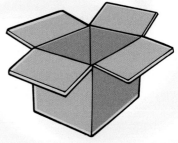

3.1 Reversible and irreversible changes

Reversible changes

Words to learn

reversible

irreversible

Activity 3.1

Observing changes to ice

Place the ice cubes in the sun or other warm place for five minutes.

What has happened to the ice after five minutes?

What causes the ice to change?

What will happen to the ice if you put it back in the freezer? Why?

You will need:

ice cubes • saucer • watch

In a warm place the solid ice becomes liquid water. When you put the ice back in the freezer it becomes a solid again. We say that the changes are **reversible** because we can change solid ice back to liquid water and liquid water back to solid ice. Heat causes the ice to melt. When the water loses heat and cools it becomes solid again. This diagram shows phase changes between ice and water

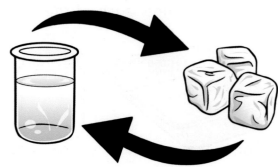

Irreversible changes

When some substances are heated, the changes cannot be reversed. We call these **irreversible** changes. Sometimes irreversible changes turn one substance into another substance. For example, when we burn a match the wood changes into a black substance called carbon.

What happens when we burn a match? Can the match change back to the way it was?

Questions

1 When you mix boiling water with jelly powder, the mixture is a liquid. In the fridge it becomes solid. Can we make jelly change back to a liquid? Draw a simple flow diagram to explain your answer.

2 **a** Does boiling an egg cause a reversible or irreversible change? Explain why.

   b Does a new substance form when you boil an egg?

3 Think of an irreversible change that forms a new substance.

Glass can be collected in recycling centres and used again.

What you have learnt

🌀 Heat makes substances change.

🌀 Some changes are reversible, for example, ice melting and refreezing.

🌀 Some changes are irreversible, for example, burning a match.

🌀 Some changes cause a new substance to form.

Talk about it!

How is glass recycled to form new glass products?

3.2 Mixing and separating solids

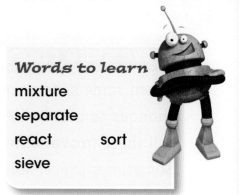

What is a mixture?

A **mixture** is made up of two or more different substances mixed together. The substances in a mixture are not chemically joined and so we can **separate** them. Mixtures can be solids, liquids or gases. Air is mixture of three main gases: nitrogen, oxygen and carbon dioxide. Think of some other mixtures.

Activity 3.2a

Making mixtures of solids

Make the following mixtures in separate jars:

- rice and flour
- salt and sand
- tea leaves and sugar
- beans and marbles.

Stir each mixture well.
Observe the mixtures.
Can you see the different substances in each mixture?
Have the substances in each mixture changed in any way?

You will need:
rice • flour • salt • sand
tea leaves • sugar • beans
marbles • glass jars • spoons

Rice and flour   Salt and sand   Tea leaves and sugar   Beans and marbles

The substances in a mixture do not change when they are mixed together.
We say that they do not **react** with each other.

Separating mixtures

We can separate the substances in mixtures in different ways.

If you pick out the nuts in a mixture of nuts and raisins, then you **sort** the mixture. Gardeners use a **sieve** to separate stones from the soil.

Peanuts and raisins are a mixture of solids. If you don't like raisins you can pick out the nuts.

Activity 3.2b

Investigating separating mixtures of solids

Select a method to separate each of the mixtures.
You can choose sieving or sorting.
Separate the mixtures.

You will need:
the mixtures from Activity 3.2a • sieve glass jars • bowl

Questions

1   Were there any mixtures you could not separate? If so, why do you think this happened?

2   Which method is best for separating mixtures that contain:
    a large particles that you can see easily?
    b small particles that you cannot see easily?

3   Predict, with reasons, which method of separation is best for separating mixtures of:
    a peanuts and beans
    b salt and breadcrumbs
    c peas and flour.

Talk about it!
How can scrap yards separate iron from a mixture of different scrap metals?

What you have learnt

🌀 A mixture is made up of two or more different substances mixed together.

🌀 The substances in a mixture do not react with one another.

🌀 Some solids can be mixed and separated again by sorting and sieving.

3.3 Soluble and insoluble substances

Some solids like sugar can **dissolve** in a liquid. Sugar can dissolve in water. It is called a **soluble** substance.

Some solids do not dissolve in a liquid. Sand does not dissolve in water. We say it is **insoluble** in water.

Words to learn
dissolve
soluble
insoluble
suspension

What happens to the sugar that we stir into our tea?

Activity 3.3

Investigating soluble and insoluble substances

Look at all the solids that your teacher provided. Predict which substances will be soluble in water. Write down your predictions in a table like this.

You will need:
measuring cylinder
glass jars • teaspoon
clean water • different solids

Substance	Prediction: soluble or insoluble?	Observation: clear or cloudy?	Conclusion: soluble or insoluble?

Measure 100 ml of water into each jar.

Add one teaspoon of solid to each jar.

Stir the water and observe what happens. Are the mixtures clear or cloudy?

Can you still see the solid substance?

Record your observations and conclusions in the table.

Leave the mixtures for five minutes and observe them again.

Questions

1 a What happened to the solids in the cloudy mixtures?

   b What happened to the solids in the clear mixtures?

2 a What happened to the mixtures after five minutes

   b Why do you think this happened?

3 Which substances dissolved in the water? Were your predictions correct?

4 Why is it important to use the same amount of water and solid in every case?

Soluble substances mix completely with the liquid so that you cannot see them.

When you mix insoluble solids in a liquid you can still see the solid.

An insoluble solid forms a **suspension** in a liquid.

What you have learnt

- Substances that dissolve in liquids are soluble.
- Substances that do not dissolve in liquids are insoluble.
- Soluble substances mix completely with the liquid so that you cannot see them.
- Insoluble substances do not mix with the liquid and form a suspension.

Talk about it!

Why do lumps of sugar dissolve slower than grains of sugar?

3.4 Separating insoluble substances

Words to learn

filtering

filter

wetland

What is filtering?

Filtering is a method used to separate mixtures of a solid and liquid. A **filter** works like a sieve. A filter separates soluble and insoluble substances. It has tiny holes that let through very small particles but not bigger particles. The liquid and the soluble substances dissolved in the liquid pass through the holes. Insoluble solid particles are too big to pass through and stay behind. For example, the filter paper in a coffee pot lets the water through but not the grains of coffee.

Sand filters use layers of gravel and fine sand to separate particles of solids from water.

In nature wetlands such as marshes and swamps acts as filters. As water passes through the **wetland** it slows down. The soil and gravel of the wetland filter out particles of different substances from the water. Some of these substances may be harmful, for example chemicals and human body wastes. The wetland makes the water cleaner.

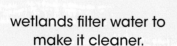

wetlands filter water to make it cleaner.

3 Material changes

Activity 3.4

Separating mixtures by filtering

Measure 100 ml of water into each jar.
Stir one teaspoon of solid into each jar.
Use the filter funnel and filter paper to filter each mixture into another jar

Questions

1   What was left behind on the filter paper after you filtered each mixture?

2   What went through the filter paper into the container? Why did this happen?

3   Can you separate the solid and liquid in a solution by filtering? Say why or why not.

4   **a** Predict the results you would obtain if you filter a mixture of flour and water.

   b Give a reason for your prediction.

Challenge

Design a method to separate a mixture of sand and salt.

Flamingoes and many other birds have filters in their beaks. They catch food like algae and small fish by filtering the water.

What you have learnt

🌀 Filtering separates insoluble solids from liquids in mixtures.

🌀 In a filter, very small particles pass through tiny holes in the filter, but bigger particles cannot pass through.

Talk about it!

How does a teabag let the flavour and colour of the tea through, but keep the tea leaves behind?

3.5 Solutions

Words to learn
solution
solute
solvent
uniform

You have found out that some substances can dissolve in water or other liquids. These substances are soluble. A soluble substance forms a **solution** with a liquid. Solutions always have two parts:

- the substance that dissolves, called the **solute**
- the liquid in which the solute dissolves, called the **solvent**.

Look at the picture of seawater. Can you see the salt in the water? How do you know the water contains salt if you can't see it?

Seawater is a solution. The salt dissolves in the water to make the solution. The salt is the solute and the water is the solvent.

Activity 3.5

Making a solution

Pour 100 ml of water into the jar.
Put a teaspoon of crystals into the jar and observe what happens.
What can you observe in the water around the crystals?
Draw and label your observations.
Wait five minutes. Can you see the solid crystals anymore?
In this activity, which is the solute and which is the solvent?

You will need:
water • coloured crystals
glass jar • teaspoon
measuring cylinder • watch

The particles of the solute move between the solvent particles when they dissolve. Because of this you cannot see the solute in a solution after it has dissolved. We say that a solution has a **uniform** appearance. It looks the same throughout.

Mixtures and pure substances

Mixtures are made of particles of different substances. We can separate most mixtures because the particles of the substances in the mixture are not chemically joined together. A pure substance consists only of particles of that substance. The particles in pure substances are chemically joined together and cannot be separated.

Powder for a cool drink is a mixture. It is made of particles of sugar and other substances.

Solute particles spread out evenly in the solvent.

Sugar is a pure substance. It is made only of particles of sugar.

Questions

1   Is a solution a mixture or a pure substance? Discuss this question and make a prediction about the answer.

2   What evidence do you need to collect to investigate the question and why?

3   How could you make sure you collect enough evidence?

4   What equipment and methods would you use?

5   How would you make your test a fair test?

What you have learnt

- A solution is made up of a solute dissolved in a solvent.
- Mixtures are made of particles of different substances. Pure substances consist only of particles of that substance.
- Most mixtures can be separated but pure substances cannot be separated.

Talk about it!

Is the juice of an orange a mixture, solution or a pure substance?

Words to learn

rate

conclude

Why do you think the coffee tasted bitter? How could the boy make the coffee taste sweeter without adding any more sugar?

The coffee and sugar form a solution. The sugar will dissolve faster if the boy stirs the solution. Stirring is one way to make solid solutes dissolve faster. Stirring causes the particles of the solute to spread out into the spaces between the particles of the solvent more quickly. We say that stirring increases the rate at which a solute dissolves.

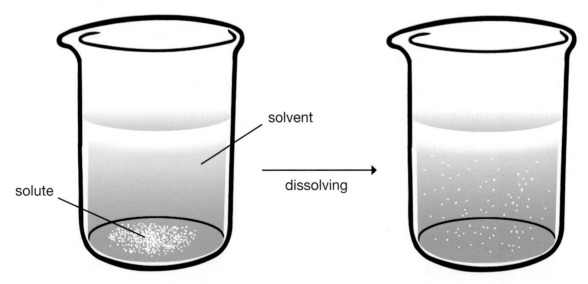

When a solute dissolves, the particles spread out through the solvent. This happens more quickly if you stir.

There are other factors that make solids dissolve faster. Have you ever tried to make coffee with water from the fridge? Why do we use hot water?

Activity 3.6

Does sugar dissolve more quickly in hot or cold water?

Does sugar dissolve more quickly in hot or cold water? Make a prediction.

Stir a teaspoon of sugar into 100 ml of cold water in a glass jar.

Stir a teaspoon of sugar into 100 ml of hot water in a glass jar.

Time how long it takes for the sugar to dissolve in both jars.

Record your results in a table.

Questions

1 a In which jar did the sugar dissolve quickest? Suggest a reason for this.
   b Was your prediction correct?
2 How did you make sure that your test was fair?
3 Write down what you **conclude** about the effect of temperature on dissolving a solute.

The particles in matter are always moving. When we increase the temperature of a substance, the heat adds energy to the particles of the substance. This energy causes them to move faster.

In a heated solvent, the particles of the solute move faster than in a cooler solvent. This allows the particles of the solute to spread through the solution more easily, so the solute dissolves faster.

What you have learnt

🌀 Stirring a solution makes solid solutes dissolve faster. This is because the particles of solute spread out into the spaces between the particles of the solvent more quickly.

🌀 Heating a solution makes solid solutes dissolve faster. This is because heat speeds up the particles and allows the solute to spread through the solution more easily.

Talk about it!
Do all solutes dissolve faster in hot water?

3.7 How does grain size affect dissolving?

Activity 3.7

Does grain size affect the rate of dissolving?

Do large grains dissolve faster than small grains? Write down a prediction.

Plan and conduct an investigation to find out.

Make a list of all the materials and equipment you need.

Identify the factors you are going to change.

List all the factors that you are going keep the same.

Write down a method that you can follow to carry out a fair test.

Record your results in a table.

Draw a bar chart of your results.

coarse salt with large grains   fine salt with small grains

Questions

1 Does the evidence you obtained support your prediction? How?

2 What conclusion can you draw from your results?

3 Suggest a way to check if your conclusion is correct.

4 Predict how the time taken for the grains to dissolve would change if you used a fine powder.

The grain size of a solute affects the rate at which it will dissolve in a liquid. Each small grain is made of fewer particles than each large grain. The particles on the outside of the grain dissolve first because they are in contact with the liquid. When they dissolve, other particles in the grain come in contact with the liquid and dissolve. In large grains with lots of particles, it takes longer for all the particles to come into contact with the liquid and dissolve.

Rainwater can dissolve some types of rock. When the rainwater falls through a cave, some of the rock particles can come out of the solution, forming dripstones like these.

What you have learnt

🌀 The grain size of a solute affects the rate at which it will dissolve in a liquid.

🌀 Small grains dissolve faster than large grains.

Talk about it!

Why do you think we dissolve some medicines, such as aspirin tablets?

1. Sunil made popcorn. He heated oil in a cooking pot and put in the popcorn kernels. A minute later they popped to make popcorn.

   a Is this a reversible or irreversible change? Say why.
   b What makes the popcorn kernels change?
   c Did a new substance form? Say why or why not.
   d Draw a flow diagram to show the change in the popcorn.

2. These are pictures of mixtures.

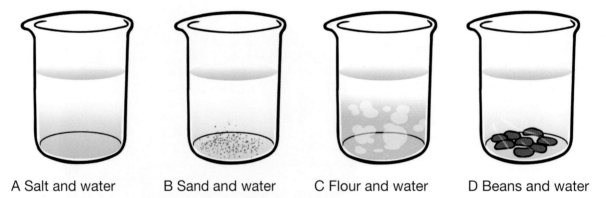

   A Salt and water   B Sand and water   C Flour and water   D Beans and water

   a Which substances in the mixtures are soluble and which are insoluble?
   b Which mixture is a solution? How do you know this?
   c Which mixture is a suspension? How do you know this?
   d How can you separate Mixture B?
   e Name two ways you can separate Mixture D.

3 When you make jelly you mix jelly powder with water to make a solution.

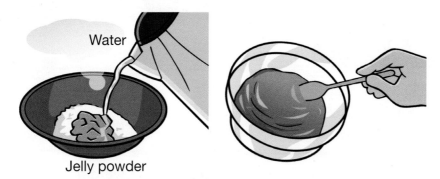

Water

Jelly powder

a Name the solute in the jelly solution.

b Name the solvent in the jelly solution.

c Make a drawing to show the dissolved particles in the jelly solution.

d Name two factors that affect the rate of dissolving when you make jelly.

3 Arrange the steps of an investigation in the correct order. Write the letter of the sentences, **A–G**, in the correct order.

A I have learned that sand cannot dissolve in water.

B I put one teaspoon full of sand into the water and stirred it.

C I poured some water into the jar.

D I decided which materials and equipment I needed for my experiment.

E After ten minutes, the sand formed a layer at the bottom of the bottle.

F I asked the question: How can I find out if sand dissolves in water?

G I found a glass jar, a teaspoon and a cup of sand.

4 Forces and motion

4.1 Mass and weight

What is the difference between mass and weight?

Is the boy in the picture correct?

Mass is the amount of matter in an object. We measure mass in units such as grams and **kilograms**. The boy's mass is 35 kg, but what is his **weight**?

I weigh 35 kilograms

Mass and weight are not the same. To understand what weight is, you need to think about the **force** of **gravity**. What happens when you drop a book?

All objects are attracted to the Earth by gravity. The bigger the mass of the object, the bigger is the force of attraction towards the Earth. Weight is the amount of attraction on an object caused by gravity. Objects with a bigger mass therefore have a bigger weight.

We measure weight using a unit called the **newton** (N). Newtons are named after Sir Isaac Newton, a scientist who lived in England about 400 years ago. He was the first person to explain what forces are.

Measuring mass and weight

Mass and weight are different, so we measure them in different ways.

Which do you think has the larger mass, 10 g of feathers or 10 g of sand?

We use scales like these to measure mass and

Words to learn

mass

kilogram

weight

force

gravity

newton

Measuring mass and weight

Make a table to record your measurements using the scales to measure mass and the measurements using the forcemeter.

On the table, write in the units used to measure the readings on the scales to measure mass and the readings on the forcemeter to measure weight.

Place each of the objects, one at a time, on the scales. Record your measurements in the table.

Then hang the forcemeter on a door handle or hold it in your hand.

Put each of the objects, one at a time, in the plastic bag.

Hang the bag on the forcemeter.

Record your measurements in the table.

You will need:
objects of different masses
plastic carrier bag
scale to measure mass
forcemeter

We use forcemeters to measure weight.

Questions

1   Compare the readings on the weighing scales with the readings on the forcemeter. What pattern do you notice?

What you have learnt

- Mass is the amount of matter in an object.
- Weight is the amount of force that pulls objects towards the Earth.
- We measure mass in kilograms and weight in newtons.
- One kilogram of mass has a force of ten newtons on Earth.

Talk about it!
Why do astronauts float in space?

An astronaut on a spacewalk.

4.2 How forces act

When we drop a book it falls to the ground. Gravity pulls all objects downwards. But can forces act in other directions?

What forces can you identify in the picture?

Activity 4.2

Investigating direction of forces

Put the book on the table. Does it move?

What would happen to the book if the table wasn't there? Why?

Hook one end of the elastic band around your forefinger. Pull on the other end of the elastic band. In which direction does the elastic band move? Why?

Name the force acting on the elastic band.

Hold the magnet above the nail. In which direction does the nail move? Why?

Name the force acting on the nail.

You will need:
a book • a table
an elastic band • a magnet
an iron nail

Forces can act in different directions. When you put the book on the table, the book will **exert** a downward force on the table. This force is caused by gravity pulling the book downwards. The force is the weight of the book. The reason the book doesn't fall is because the table exerts an upwards force on the book.

Force diagrams

We can show the direction of forces on an object in a drawing called a **force diagram**. Each force is shown as a force arrow. When the forces are equal, the force arrows are the same length

Downwards force of book on table

Upwards force of table on book

Forces always act in pairs. In the picture, the book exerts a downward force on the table and the table exerts an upward force on the book. The two forces act in opposite directions.

Questions

1 a Copy the drawing and add arrows to show the direction in which each of the forces act.

   b Is one force bigger than the other? Say why or why not.

2 When you stand still, why don't you sink into the ground? Draw a force diagram to explain your answer.

What you have learnt

- Forces act in different directions.
- Forces act in pairs. Each force in a force pair acts in the opposite direction to the other.
- Force diagrams show the direction and size of forces.

Talk about it!
Why does a boat float on the water?

A Vietnamese coracle.

4.3 Balanced and unbalanced forces

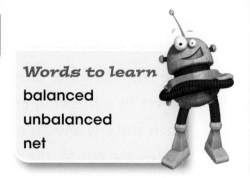

Words to learn
balanced
unbalanced
net

Activity 4.3

Which force is bigger?

Stretch out your arm and hold up the book.
Does the book move?
What happens if you hold
the book for two minutes?

You will need:
a heavy book • a watch

Questions

1 a What force is acting on the book?
   b What force is acting on your arm?
   c When you first hold up the book,
     is one force bigger than the other?
     Say why or why not.
2 After holding the book for two
   minutes, is one force bigger than the
   other? Say why or why not.

Remember that forces act in pairs. When
you are holding a book, you use an
upward force to hold up the book. The
book exerts a downward force, caused
by gravity pulling the book downwards.
The forces are the same size but in
opposite directions. When both forces
are the same size the object does not
move. We say the forces are **balanced**.

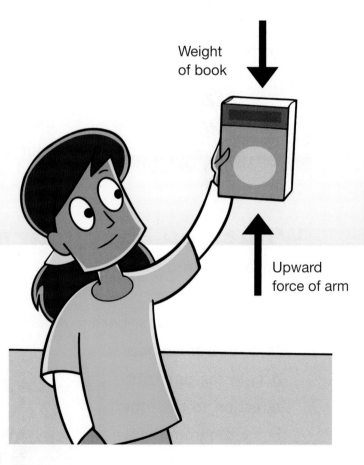

Weight
of book

Upward
force of arm

As your arm gets tired, you exert less upward force. The book exerts a bigger force than your arm, so your arm drops a bit. If one force is bigger than the other, an object moves in the direction of the force. The two forces are **unbalanced**. The arrows in the picture show the size of the forces: the longer the arrow, the bigger the force.

When forces are unbalanced and one force is greater than the other, we say there is a **net** force. When forces are balanced we say there is no net force.

Weight of book

Upward force of arm

Neither side is winning. Are the forces balanced?

What you have learnt

- 🌀 When both forces on an object are the same size, the forces are balanced.
- 🌀 When one force on an object is bigger than the opposite force, the forces are unbalanced.
- 🌀 When two opposite forces are not balanced, there is a net force.

Talk about it!

Why can a flying golf ball break a window but a ping pong ball can't?

4.4 The effects of forces

We cannot see forces, but we can see or feel what they can do.

Activity 4.4

Investigating what forces do

Put the ball on the table. Does the ball move?

Blow on the ball through the straw.

What happens to the ball?

Hold up a book across one end of the table. Roll the ball gently towards the book.

Allow the ball to roll into the book. What happens to the ball?

Flick the ball with your fingers towards someone in your group.

Get that group member to flick the ball to someone else.

What happens to the direction of the ball each time you flick it?

Squeeze the ball gently.

What happens to the shape of the ball?

Are the forces in each case balanced or unbalanced?

You will need:
a ping pong ball • a straw
a table • a book

What can forces do?

Forces can make things move. When you exert a force on a ball by blowing or rolling it, you make the ball move. Forces can also speed up moving objects.

Forces can also slow down moving objects or make them stop. When the ball rolls into the book it stops moving. The book exerts a force on the ball to stop it moving.

Forces can change the direction in which an object moves. When you flick the ball from person to person, it changes direction each time. Each person exerts a force on the ball that changes the direction of the ball's movement.

Forces can change the shape of an object. When you squeeze a ball you exert a force on it. The force makes the ball change shape.

Forces that change the movement or shape of an object are unbalanced forces.

Questions

1 We cannot see forces. Name four ways we know that forces exist.
2 a How do forces act to break a glass when it falls on the ground?
  b How do forces act to make a rubber ball bounce when you drop it?

What you have learnt

- Forces change the movement of an object by speeding it up or slowing it down.
- Forces change an object's direction of movement.
- Forces change the shape of an object.

Talk about it!
Why does the front of a car crumple if it drives into a tree?

Modern cars have crumple zones which protect passengers in an accident.

4.5 Forces and energy

Words to learn

energy

work

A force is needed to make objects move or to stop them moving.

When we exert a force on an object to make it move, we give the object **energy**. The amount of energy transferred to an object to make it move is called **work**.

A force is needed to make the toy car move.

A force is needed stop the toy car moving.

How much work is done?

The amount of work done depends on how far the force makes the object move. The further the object moves, the more work is done as more energy is transferred.

The force from the boy's foot transfers energy to the ball. The ball moves and work is done.

If no force is applied to a ball it cannot move and no work is done.

If there is a force on an object but the object doesn't move, no work is done.

Questions

1 Can an object move by itself? Explain your answer.

2 When you open a door:
   a What force do you exert on it?
   b Is any work done? Say why or why not.

3 How can you increase the amount of work done when you lift a book? Explain your answer.

Challenge

Where does the energy come from to make this windmill turn?

What you have learnt

- A force is needed to make objects move or to stop them moving.
- Moving objects have energy.
- Work is the amount of energy transferred to an object to make it move.

Talk about it!
Where do you get energy from to make objects move?

4.6 Friction

Activity 4.6

What is friction?

Rub your hands together for 30 seconds.
How do your hands feel? Are they warmer?

You will need:
a watch

Friction is a force which tries to stop things sliding past one another. Friction is caused when two surfaces rub together.

Friction only acts on moving objects and it cannot make objects move. Friction slows down moving objects. Friction changes the energy of moving objects into heat energy as the objects slow down.

How is friction useful?

You could not walk without friction between your shoes and the ground.

Friction holds your shoe to the ground, allowing you to walk. Think how difficult it is to walk on ice or a wet, slippery floor, where there is little friction.

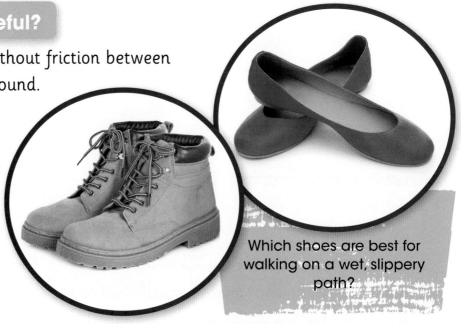

Which shoes are best for walking on a wet, slippery path?

You could not hold a pencil in your hand without friction. It would slip out when you tried to hold it to write. The pencil lead would not make a mark on the paper without friction.

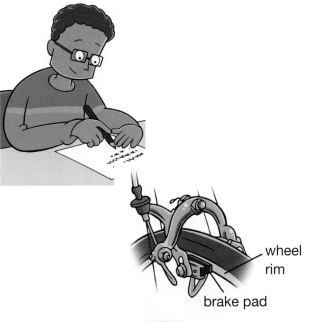

The brakes in cars, bicycles and other vehicles use friction to slow down and stop. When you pull the brake lever of a bicycle, the brake pads of the bicycle push on the rim of the wheel. This creates friction which makes the wheel turn more slowly.

wheel rim

brake pad

How is friction a problem?

Friction makes things wear out.

Because friction causes heat, moving parts in machines get hot when they rub together. Oil is needed to lubricate the machines and allow their parts to move easily. The oil forms a thin layer on the surface of the parts so they don't rub together as much.

Friction between a car's tyres and the road make the tyres wear out.

Questions

1 How do we use friction to clean our clothes?
2 Think of **two** examples of friction making things we use everyday wear out.
3 How is friction different from other forces?
4 How can we reduce friction?

Challenge

Is there any friction in space? Why or why not?

What you have learnt

- Friction is a force that stops things sliding past each other.
- Friction slows down moving objects.
- Friction can be useful as it helps objects to grip on surfaces.
- Friction can be a problem as it makes objects wear out and get hot.

Talk about it!

How does a pencil eraser work?

4.7 Investigating friction

Some surfaces are more slippery than others. Why?

Activity 4.7

How does a surface affect friction?

Set up the plank so that it makes a slope.

You will need:
a plank of wood
a pile of books • liquid soap
sand • water
a matchbox filled with sand
a shoebox • a stop watch

Put the matchbox at the top of the slope.

Measure how fast in seconds the matchbox moves down the slope.

Repeat the measurements another three times.

Record your results in a table like this one.

Time taken for matchbox to reach ground in seconds	Wood	Wood covered in soap
reading 1		

Cover the plank with liquid soap.

Put the matchbox at the top of the slope.

Measure how fast the matchbox moves down the slope. Repeat the measurements another three times.

Pour sand from the matchbox into a shoebox. Predict whether the shoebox will move faster down the plank than the matchbox.

Test your prediction on the dry wood and the soapy wood surfaces.

Questions

1 Compare the results for the two surfaces. On which surface did the matchbox move faster?

2 Which surface exerted the bigger frictional force? How do you know this?

3 How did the soap change the surface of the wood?

4 Why is it good to repeat measurements?

5 **a** Suggest a reason for your prediction. Think about which box has the bigger surface area.

   b Why did you pour the sand from the matchbox into the shoebox?

   c Suggest a reason for the results you obtained when you tested your prediction on the dry wood and soapy surfaces. Was your prediction correct?

6 Name **two** factors that affect frictional forces between two surfaces.

Ball bearings.

What you have learnt

🌀 Frictional force is greater between rough surfaces than between smooth surfaces.

🌀 Frictional force is bigger over large surfaces than small surfaces.

Talk about it!

How do ball bearings in machines reduce friction?

4.8 Air resistance and drag

Words to learn
air resistance
drag
surface area

Have you ever held your hand out of a car window? What did you feel?

Air is a mixture of gases. The particles of gas push against things which are moving and create a force. This force is called air resistance. Another name for it is drag. Air resistance pushes against a moving object such as a car and slows it down. The larger the surface area of the moving object, the more air resistance there is.

Air resistance also pushes against falling objects and slows them down. A parachute uses air resistance to work. It is very light in weight and has a very big surface area. It catches lots of air in it as it falls down so it creates a lot of air resistance or drag.

Which has the greater air resistance, the pick-up or the lorry?

Making a parachute

Cut out a square from the plastic bag.

Trim the edges so it looks like an octagon (an eight-sided shape).

Cut a small hole near the edge of each side.

Thread a piece of string through each of the holes. The strings should be of the same length.

With sticky tape join the strings to the object you are using as a weight.

Stand on a chair to drop your parachute. Remember that you want it to drop as slowly as possible.

Record the time for the parachute to reach the ground.

Check your results by dropping the parachute another three times. Record these results in a table.

You will need:
string • plastic bag
sticky tape • weights
scissors • watch

Questions

1 a Name **two** forces that acted on your parachute.
   b Draw a force diagram to show the forces acting on the parachute.
2 a Calculate the average time it took your parachute to fall.
   b Suggest a way you could change your parachute to make it fall more slowly.
3 Would your parachute fall faster or slower if you tested it outside on a windy day? Give a reason for your answer.

The space shuttle lands with a parachute attached.

What you have learnt

- Air resistance is a force caused by air pushing against moving objects.
- Air resistance is bigger over large surfaces.

Talk about it!

Why does a space shuttle have a parachute attached to it when it lands?

1 Name the type of force acting in each of these pictures.

2 When an astronaut stands on a weighing scales on Earth, they read 60 kg. The astronaut travels to planet X which has half the gravitational force of the Earth.

    a What is the astronaut's mass on Earth?

    b What is her weight on Earth?

    c What is her mass on planet X?

    d What is her weight on planet X?

3 Describe **four** ways in which the picture shows the effects of forces on objects.

4   **a** Draw a force diagram to show the forces acting in this picture.

  b Are the forces balanced or unbalanced? Say why.

5 Explain the reason for each the following:

  a Racing cars have smooth tyres.
  b The tyres of trucks have lots of grooves.
  c Racing cars are low, flat cars.

6 For each picture say if work is being done, or not, and why.

5 Electrical conductors and insulators

5.1 Which materials conduct electricity?

In Stage 4, you learnt about electric current. An electric current needs a continuous path. This path is called an electric circuit.

Words to learn
battery
conductor
insulator

So far you have used the word 'cells' for the energy storage units like the ones in a torch. Each cell stores 1.5 V of electricity. When we have two or more of these cells connected together we call it a battery. Cells and batteries push electricity round a circuit.

What are conductors and insulators?

The metal wire is made of copper and it carries the electricity. Materials like metals allow electricity to pass through them. A material that allows electricity to pass through it is called a conductor.

The copper wire is covered with plastic. This material does not allow electricity to pass through it. It is called an insulator.

Activity 5.1

Test materials to see if they conduct electricity

Attach wires to the cell and bulb holder

You will need:
three wires • sticky tape
a screwdriver • a 1.5 V cell
a 1.5 V bulb in a bulb holder
• objects made of different materials

Connect the third wire to the bulb holder and leave the other end free.

Check that your circuit works. Hold the bare ends of the wires together. If the bulb lights up the circuit works. Separate the ends and the bulb goes out.

Test each material. Hold the bare end of one wire at one end of the object. Hold the second bare wire at the other end.

This is your testing equipment. You will use this to see which materials allow electricity to pass though. Before you begin, predict which materials will allow electricity to pass through and which will not. Record your predictions in a table.

If the bulb does not light up, then you can try again to make sure.

Record your results in the last column of your table.

Safety

Do not touch any bare electric wires. Always hold the plastic-covered wire.

Questions

1 How well did your results support your predictions?
2 Identify which types of material are conductors and which are insulators.
3 Did any materials not fit this pattern? If so, identify the material.
4 What conclusion can you make from your results?

Talk about it!
What would happen if the wires in a circuit were not covered in plastic?

What you have learnt

- Metals conduct electricity and are called conductors.
- Other materials do not conduct electricity and are called insulators.

5.2 Does water conduct electricity?

Is water pure?

Water from a river or the tap is not **pure**. It has salts dissolved in it. Pure water is **distilled** water. This is water that has been boiled and the steam has been condensed. The condensed steam does not contain any dissolved salts.

You are going to investigate whether pure water and salty water conduct electricity.

All living things contain water. Our bodies are about 65% water! This water has substances, including salts, dissolved in it, so it is not pure.

Activity 5.2

Investigating whether water conducts electricity

You will need:
a circuit with 3V battery as shown in the picture
distilled water
two teaspoons of salt
aluminium foil

Connect up the circuit with the battery, the bulb in the bulb holder and three lengths of wire.

Fold the pieces of aluminium foil and press them to the bare ends of the wire.

Pour 250 ml of distilled water into the beaker. Dip the aluminium foil ends into the water.

Predict whether the bulb will light up.

Test the circuit by holding the bare ends of the wires together. Does the bulb light up?

Add two teaspoons of salt to the water and stir it. Now dip the aluminium foil ends into the salt water. Predict whether the bulb will light up.

Observe whether the bulb lights up.

Questions

1 Did your results support your predictions?

2 Compare the result you got with pure water and with salty water.

3 What conclusion can you make about whether water conducts electricity?

4 Would you be a good or a bad conductor of electricity? Explain why.

5 Look at the picture of Lan in the bathroom. What is she doing that is dangerous? Explain why it is dangerous.

What you have learnt

🌀 Pure water does not conduct electricity.

🌀 Water with salts dissolved in it does conduct electricity.

Talk about it!
How do you know that the water in our bodies is salty?

5.3 Do different metals conduct electricity equally well?

Measuring current

Current is the rate at which the electric charges flow. You will measure current in Activity 5.3.

We measure current by the number of charges that flow through a point in a circuit in one second. We measure current in units called **amperes** or amps for short. We use an instrument called a **multimeter** to measure current. The multimeter has **connectors**.

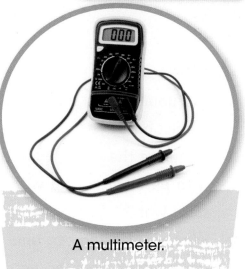

A multimeter.

Metals and alloys

Many objects are made of a combination of different metals. These are called alloys. Stainless steel is a mixture of iron, nickel and chromium. Brass is a mixture of copper and tin.

Activity 5.3

Investigating how well metals conduct electricity

Safety Do *not* touch any bare electric wires.

You will need:
plastic-covered wire
sticky tape • a screwdriver
a 1.5V cell • a multimeter
some metal objects

Set up your circuit like this. Connect the positive end of the multimeter to the positive terminal of the battery. Check that it works. Hold the plastic coated wire and let the bare end touch the connector of the multimeter. A reading on the multimeter shows that the circuit works

This is your testing equipment to see how well metals conduct electricity. Before you begin, predict which metals will be the best conductors. Record your predictions in a table.

If the multimeter doesn't show a reading first time then check again. Record your results in a table.

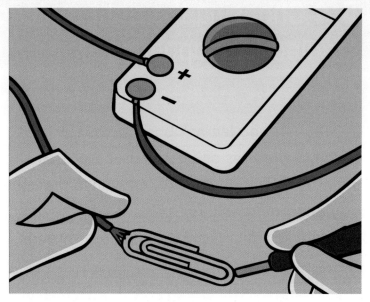

Test each metal. Hold the bare end of one wire to one end of the object. Hold the connector of the multimeter to the other end of the object. Read the current in amps on the multimeter.

Questions

1 Did all the metals conduct electricity?

2 Which metal was the best conductor? How did you know this was the best conductor?

3 How well did your results support your predictions?

4 What conclusion can you make from your results?

Challenge

Gold is a very good conductor of electricity. Why isn't gold wire used in circuits?

What you have learnt

🌀 All metals conduct electricity but some metals conduct electricity better than others.

Talk about it!
Why are lightning conductors made from copper?

5.4 Choosing the right materials for electrical appliances

Word to learn
plug

Conductors, insulators and mains electricity

In Stage 4, you learnt about mains electricity, which has a voltage of 110 V in some countries and 220 V in others. At these high voltages, safety is very important. The parts of an appliance that you touch must be made from an insulating material. The parts inside the appliance are made from conducting material so that electricity can pass through.

You saw in Activity 5.3 that metals are good electrical conductors. The parts of electrical appliances that let electricity pass through are made of metal.

For example, metal is used for the metal pins in a **plug**. The pins allow electricity to travel from the wall socket, through the plug, and into an appliance such as a kettle or television.

When we handle the plug, we only touch the cover. This is made of plastic, which is a good insulator.

Look at the diagrams. Discuss the use of conductors and insulators in these components.

A switch. You made one like this in stage 4.

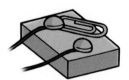

A switch cover plate for mains electricity

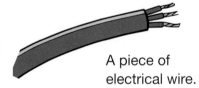

A piece of electrical wire.

Using mains electricity safely

If mains electricity flows through your body, then you will get an electric shock. You will be badly burnt, your heart could stop and you could die.

Damaged electrical wiring is a major cause of accidents with electricity. Plastic insulation often wears off the copper wires. You can get a shock if you touch the wires.

Here are two ways that electrical wires get damaged.

Never place an electric wire under a carpet. When people walk on the carpet, the plastic wears off the copper wires. When copper wires touch each other, electricity flows between them and this can start a fire.

Never pull a plug out like this. This damages the cord and the wires become bare. Grip the plug to pull it out of the socket. Turn off the switch before you pull out the plug.

Questions

1 Find appliances at home or at school that use conductors and insulators.
   a List the appliances.
   b Choose **one** example. Draw it and label the materials used. Say whether they are conductors or insulators.

2 **a** Predict what could happen to the people in Picture A and Picture B.
   b Explain why this could happen.

3 Make a safety poster warning people about the dangers of electricity.

A

B

What you have learnt

🌀 Electrical appliances are made up of materials that conduct electricity and insulating materials that do not conduct electricity.

🌀 Knowing about electrical conductors and insulators helps us to use electricity safely.

Talk about it!
Talk about electrical conductors and insulators in your classroom.

5.5 Circuit symbols

So far we have shown circuits using pictures like the one on the left. This is a **series circuit**, which means there is only one path for the flow of electricity. Describe what is in this circuit.

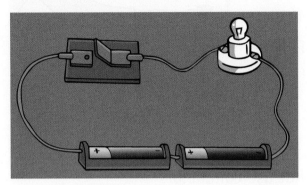

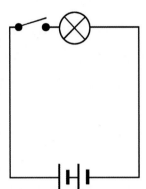

The picture on the right is a **circuit diagram** of the same circuit.

We use symbols to draw circuit diagrams. This is much quicker than drawing pictures. People all over the world can understand circuit diagrams because everyone uses the same symbols.

Here is a list of circuit components and their symbols.

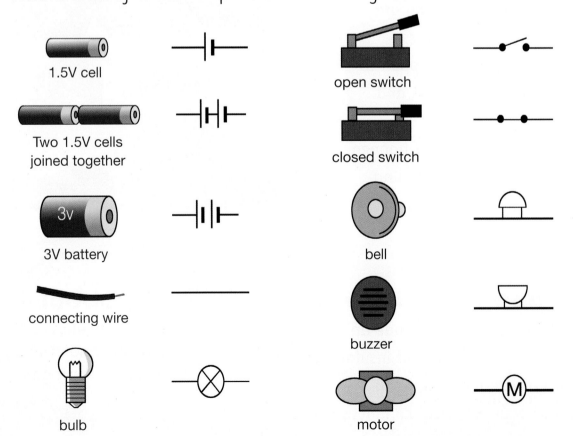

Questions

1 Look at circuit diagrams A, B and C.

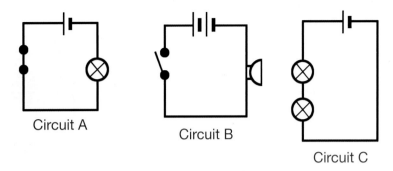

Circuit A

Circuit B

Circuit C

  a Identify the circuit that shows:

    i a battery, a buzzer and a switch.

    ii a cell, a bulb and a switch.

    iii a cell and two bulbs.

  b Which circuit shows the switch open?

  c Which circuit has the biggest energy source? How do you know?

2 Draw a circuit diagram to represent the circuit on the right.

3 Draw a circuit diagram to show a circuit with a 3 V battery, two bulbs and a closed switch.

What you have learnt

🔹 Circuit symbols represent the components of an electric circuit.

🔹 A circuit diagram shows where components are found in the circuit.

Talk about it!

What other symbols do we use every day when we communicate?

Some circuits have lots of components.

Activity 5.6a

Making a circuit with more components

Make the circuit using one of the bulbs as shown in this diagram.

Close the switch. Observe the bulb.

Open the switch.

Predict what would happen if you add one more bulb in a bulb holder to the circuit.

Test your prediction.

Did the bulbs shine more brightly or less brightly when you added a second bulb? Why?

You will need:
a 1.5V cell • two bulbs in bulb holders • a switch 150 cm wire • a sharp knife scissors • sticky tape

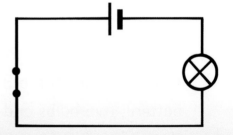

Activity 5.6b

Discussing and planning your own investigation

Here are two questions for you to test.

1 If you remove a bulb from a circuit with two 1.5 V cells joined to make a 3 V battery and three bulbs, will the bulbs glow more brightly or less brightly?

2 If you add a third 1.5 V cell to the same circuit you used in 1, will the two bulbs glow more brightly or less brightly?

Discuss how you will plan an investigation to answer these two questions. Choose what components you need to make your circuit.

Use your knowledge of electrical circuits to predict what will happen when you carry out the tests.

Make your circuit. Observe what happens when you remove the bulb and then when you add another cell. Does the evidence support the predictions you made?

Repeat any observations that you are not sure of.

Use your results to answer the questions that you were asked to test.

Questions

1   Draw a circuit diagram for each of the circuits you made in Activity 5.6b.

2   Look at Circuit A and Circuit B.
    Predict in which circuit the bulbs will be brighter.

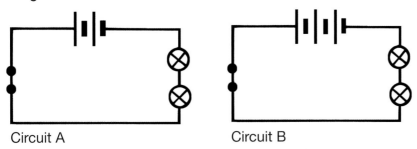

Circuit A   Circuit B

3   Suggest another circuit question that you could investigate.

What you have learnt

🌀 Removing or adding bulbs from a circuit causes them to glow more or less brightly.

🌀 Adding or removing cells used in a circuit causes bulbs to glow more or less brightly.

Talk about it!

If a circuit doesn't work, what must you check?

5.7 Adding different components

Different components need different strengths of electricity. You can put buzzers, bells and motors in a circuit instead of a bulb. These components need a stronger supply of electricity than a bulb.

Voltages

The strength of electricity is measured in a unit called a volt (V). The strength of electricity that a component needs for it to work is called the voltage. Look at the voltage of these components:

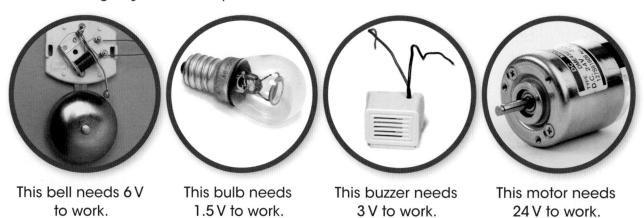

| This bell needs 6 V to work. | This bulb needs 1.5 V to work. | This buzzer needs 3 V to work. | This motor needs 24 V to work. |

If you put a 3 V buzzer into a circuit you need a 3 V battery to make the buzzer work. You can make a 3 V supply by joining two 1.5 V cells.

Activity 5.7

Building circuits using different components

You will need:
two batteries • a switch
a buzzer • connecting wires
a motor • a bell

Plan and build a circuit with a battery, a switch and a buzzer.

Test whether adding another battery will make the buzzer sound louder.

Decide how you will change the circuit if you replace the buzzer with a motor or a bell.

Discuss how you will make the circuits. Choose what components you need.

Predict what will happen before you make each circuit.

Make your first circuit. Does the buzzer work?

Add another cell to the battery. Observe any differences.

Make the changes you planned to replace the buzzer with a motor or a bell.

Predict what will happen. Does the evidence support the predictions you made?

Repeat any observations that you are not sure of.

Questions

1 Draw a circuit diagram for each of the circuits you made in Activity 5.7.

2 Think about when you added an extra cell to the battery in your buzzer circuit.
   What was your conclusion about the effect of this?

3 Look at Circuits A, B and C. The bell and buzzer need 6 V to work and the motor needs only 1.5 V.
   a Predict which of these circuits will work.
   b Explain why the other circuit does not work.

Circuit A

Circuit B

Circuit C

What you have learnt

- Different components need different strengths of electricity to work.
- Changing the number of cells affects how well components work.

Talk about it!
What do you think a 1.5 V and a 12 V motor could be used for?

5.8 Length and thickness of wire in a circuit

Look at the children watering the garden. The **pressure** of water coming from the taps is the same for each of the four hosepipes. The hosepipes supply different amounts of **resistance** to the water passing through them. If there is a lot of resistance in the hosepipe, less water comes out than if there is not much resistance in the hosepipe.

Sam has a long hosepipe and Pumla has a short hosepipe. Their hosepipes are the same thickness. Look at the long hosepipe and the short one. Which has the most water coming out? Which hosepipe offers the most resistance to the water, the long one or the short one?

Vusi has a thin hosepipe and Mary has a fat hosepipe. Their hosepipes are the same length.

Which has the most water coming out? Which offers the most resistance to the water, the thin one or the fat one?

You can apply what you know about water flow in hosepipes to electric current flow in wires.

Changing the thickness of wire in a circuit

Set up a circuit as shown in the diagram.
Insert 10 cm of thin resistance wire into the circuit.
Measure the current on the multimeter.
Now replace the thin resistance wire with the same length of thick resistance wire. But before you do this, predict whether the multimeter reading will be higher or lower.
Test your prediction.
Do you think changing the length of resistance wire will change the multimeter reading? Discuss how to test this and how much evidence you will need.
Test your prediction.

You will need:
two 1.5V cells • wire (thick and thin resistance wire)
a multimeter • crocodile clips

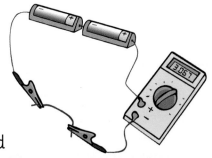

Questions

1 a Copy this sentence, choosing the correct word where there is a choice.
   Long or thin hosepipes give more/less resistance to water flow than short or fat hosepipes.

   b Write a similar sentence about the flow of electricity through different wires.

2 a How did changing the resistance wire from thin to thick change the multimeter reading?

   b Explain why this happened.

3 a How did changing the length of resistance wire change the multimeter reading?

   b Explain why this happened.

Challenge

Extension cables are often 30 m long. Why are these cables made of thick wire rather than thin wire?

An extension cable.

What you have learnt

⟳ Changing the length or thickness of wire in a circuit will change the strength of current.

Talk about it!
How has thin wire been put to good use in a light bulb?

5.9 How scientists invented batteries

All the circuits you have made have included a cell or a battery. These batteries contain chemical substances that react together. This reaction supplies the energy needed to push the electricity round the circuit. How did scientists make this discovery?

The Baghdad battery

In June 1936 workers found an ancient tomb while they were constructing a new railway near the city of Baghdad, in present-day Iraq. Archaeologists identified things in the tomb to be 2000 years old. At this time people called the Parthians lived in this region.

One of the old objects or relics they found in the tomb was a clay jar. The jar had an iron rod coming out of the centre, surrounded by a tube made of copper. Scientists made copies of it relic. When they filled the tube with an acid such as vinegar, it produced between 1.5 and 2 volts of electricity between the iron and copper. Archaeologists think that people who lived 2000 years ago could have used batteries like this to cover metal objects with gold.

Galvani's discovery

Luigi Galvani was an Italian doctor. About 1780 he discovered current electricity. He hung a frog's leg on copper hooks over an iron railing and noted that the leg muscles twitched. Galvani was correct when he said that the twitchings were caused by electrical current, but he thought that the current came from the frog's leg nerves and called it "animal electricity."

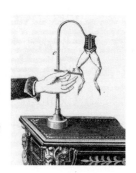

The voltaic pile

Alessandro Volta was an Italian university professor. He repeated Galvani's experiments many times with different materials. From these experiments he came to the conclusion that it was the two different metals, copper and iron, not the frog's leg that produced the electricity.

The frog's leg contained a fluid which conducted the current. It twitched because the electricity was flowing through it.

In 1800, after many experiments, he developed a type of battery that he called the voltaic pile. This consisted of a pile of zinc and copper discs. Between each disc there was a piece of cardboard that he had soaked in salt water. A wire connecting the bottom zinc disc to the top copper disc could produce a continuous flow of sparks.

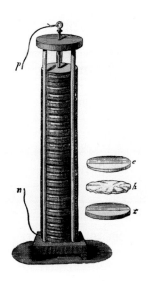

Volta built different piles using thirty, forty or sixty discs. He measured the reaction with different numbers of discs and discovered that the electric shock increased in intensity with the number of discs he used in the pile.

Later, scientists improved Volta's battery by doing more experiments.

Questions

1 What did Galvani observe in his experiments with frog's legs?
2 What did these observations lead Galvani to conclude?
3 How did Volta use creative thinking to develop Galvani's ideas further?
4 What measurements did Volta make to provide evidence for the strength of electric current?
5 Describe the differences between Galvani's and Volta's explanations for how an electric current flowed.
6 What electrical unit is named after Volta?

What you have learnt

🌀 Scientists have combined evidence from observation and measurement with creative thinking to suggest new ideas and explanations for batteries and electricity.

Talk about it!
How could people have invented batteries 2000 years ago?

5 Check your progress

1 Copy the words in column A and write their correct meanings (from column B) next to them.

Column A	Column B
ampere	a picture of a circuit using symbols
volt	a device to connect two wires together
multimeter	the unit for measuring the strength of electricity
series circuit	the unit electric current is measured in
circuit diagram	a piece of equipment for measuring current, voltage and resistance
resistance	a device for connecting an electric wire or cable to an electricity supply
connector	a circuit where the electricity only has one path to flow along
plug	the amount of restriction of flow of electricity

2 What is the difference between:

    a a cell and a battery

    b an electrical conductor and an electrical insulator

    c pure water and distilled water?

3 Draw a circuit diagram including these components to make the circuit:

> 4.5 V battery   connecting wire   switch   two bulbs

4 In which of the circuits A, B and C will the bulb not light up?

Explain your answer.

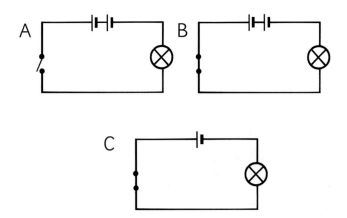

5 Explain why plug covers are made of plastic and electrical wire is made of copper.

6 Identify **two** dangers in the use of mains electricity in the picture.

How to plan an investigation

Making an idea into a question

Amna wants to test her idea. She makes it into a question 'Does stirring make sugar dissolve more quickly?'.

Choosing the equipment

They decide to dissolve the sugar in hot water and use clear containers. They put the containers onto black card. This will help them to see the sugar.

Neta gets a stopwatch so that they can measure how long the sugar takes to dissolve.

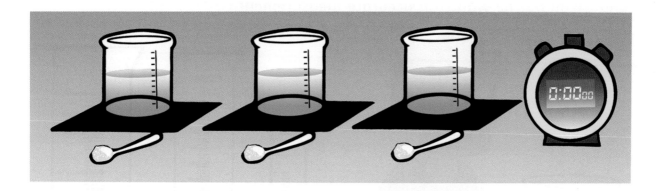

No stirring Stir 3 times every 2 minutes Stir 3 times every minute

Making the test fair

What do they need to keep the same to make the test fair?

They make a list of the variables.

Variables
Amount of sugar
Amount of water
Temperature of water
Amount of stirring

Making the test accurate

It will be hard to see exactly when all the sugar has dissolved.

We can repeat the test to make it more reliable.

It is not important who stirs the sugar in this investigation.

Choosing equipment

It is important to choose the right science equipment for an investigation.

Using the right equipment can make measurements more accurate.

Sunil wants to measure how much water he has. He can see it is between 70 and 80 ml but he wants an accurate measurement.

Sunil knows that he needs to use a measuring cylinder but he is not sure which one. Look at the water in the measuring beaker. Which measuring cylinder will give the most accurate measurement?

The 50 ml measuring cylinder is too small.

This one is best. I can see I have 73 ml water.

Sunil tries the others.

For an accurate measurement, use the smallest measuring cylinder that the liquid will fit into.

Use this page to help you choose what you need for your investigation.

scales

measuring beakers

digital timer

dropper

measuring spoons

thermometer

filter paper

sieve

bulb in holder

scales

multimeter

rulers

forcemeters

measuring cylinders

1.5 V cell

motor

funnel dropper

tape measure

Using a forcemeter

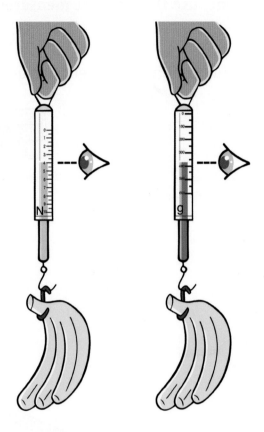

Turn the nut to check the forcemeter is set to zero.

Put the object on the forcemeter.

Put your eye level with the pointer and read the scale.

The weight of the bananas is a force of four newtons.

Many forcemeters also have a scale that will show the mass of an object in grams or kilograms.

The bananas have a mass of about 400 g.

Some forcemeters can also be used to measure the size of a pushing force.

A force of about 2.5 N is needed to push this book across the table.

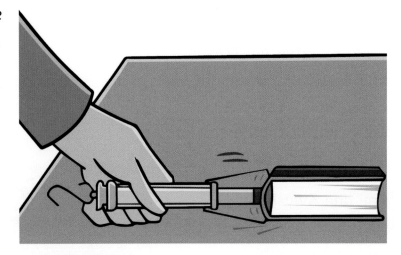

Using scales

These scales are not set to zero.

Look for a wheel at the back of the scales. Turn the wheel to set the scales to zero.

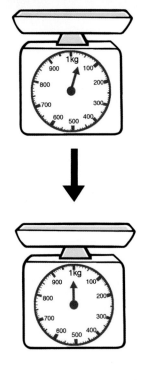

Put an object on the scales.

The scales will show the mass of the object.

This apple has a mass of 250 g.

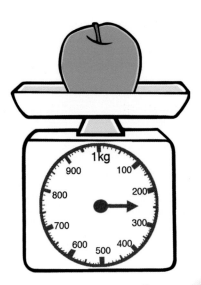

Looking for patterns in results and making conclusions

There are often patterns in results. The pattern might be results that are all the same, or it might be measurements that go up or down.

Femi and Kwasi are investigating which materials conduct electricity.

They are testing objects made from different materials. The bulb lights when the material conducts electricity.

Here are their results.

Object	Material	Bulb
scissors	metal	on
ruler	wood	off
cup	plastic	off
cup	glass	off
key	metal	on
coin	metal	on
book	paper	off
spoon	metal	on
spoon	wood	off
pencil lead	graphite	on
pen	plastic	off

Femi has seen a pattern in the results. Some of the results are the same. He uses the pattern to make a conclusion. Is Femi correct?

Metal conducts electricity. Materials that are not metal do not.

Kwasi has seen a result that does not fit the pattern.

To check that they have not made a mistake, they repeat the test with the graphite. The bulb lights up every time. So Femi's conclusion is not right.

They make new conclusions.

Some materials that are not metal do conduct electricity.

Using patterns to check that repeated measurements are reliable

Yoko and Marja are investigating how running affects pulse rate. They want to know if their pulse rate is different when they run at different speeds.

Yoko runs the same distance each time but at three different speeds.

To make their results reliable, Yoko runs at each speed three times. They measure her pulse rate after each time. They are going to take the average pulse rate for each running speed by finding the mean.

Is your pulse rate different if you run at different speeds?

Here are their results so far.

Exercise	Running very fast	Running quite fast	Running slowly
Pulse Rate 1 in beats per minute	190	102	155
Pulse Rate 2 in beats per minute	195	172	153
Pulse Rate 3 in beats per minute	188	178	210
Mean pulse rate in beats per minute			

The girls look for patterns in their results. The numbers for running very fast are almost the same. But there are two measurements in the results that could be wrong. Look for numbers that do not fit the pattern.

The girls repeat two measurements to check that they are reliable. Then they calculate the mean.

Their results now look like this.

Exercise	Running very fast	Running quite fast	Running slowly
Pulse Rate 1 in beats per minute	190	102 169	155
Pulse Rate 2 in beats per minute	195	172	153
Pulse Rate 3 in beats per minute	188	178	210 148
Mean pulse rate in beats per minute	191	173	152

Marja makes a conclusion.

The girls explain why they repeated their measurements.

The faster you run, the faster your heart beats.

When you repeat measurements it is easier to see if you have got one of them wrong.

Also, you can find the mean so your results are more reliable.

Researching questions

Sometimes a science investigation is not the best way to answer a question. You may not have the equipment you need or enough time. The answers to many questions can be found in reference books or on the internet. Mai is researching food chains.

Choosing key words

First you should think about which words to look for. These should be key words for the topic you are researching. Mai could look for *diet*, *consumer* and *prey*.

Using reference books

Scan the contents page for these words and look them up in the index.

Try looking up *consumer* and *prey* in the index to this book. Can you find out about the diet of an animal?

Using the internet

Think carefully about the words you type into a search engine. Searches for 'Crocodile diet' and 'What do crocs eat?' will list different websites.

Not all the information the internet is correct, so look carefully at the websites that come up on your search. Some are more likely to be correct than others.

Mai has found two websites with information about what crocodiles eat. Which do you think is more reliable?

To find reliable websites, look for those that come from large organisations and are written by experts. Unreliable websites often have adverts and do not look as good.

Glossary and index

conclude	to decide something is true after looking at all the evidence you have collected	53
conductor (of electricity)	a material that allows electricity to pass through it	76
connector	a device to connect two wires together	80
conserve	to keep safe, to protect from extinction	31
consumer	a living thing (usually an animal) that eats another plant or animal	24
deforestation	removal of trees by humans	30
depict	when you depict an idea you show it using a diagram or drawing	22
desert	regions with very little rainfall	28
dialysis	a way to remove wastes from the blood with a machine if the kidneys do not work properly	17
digestion	the process of breaking down food into very tiny particles	14
digestive system	the organs needed for the process of digestion including the stomach and intestines	14
disease	an illness which stops your body from working properly	17
dissolve	when a substance, often a solid, mixes with a liquid and becomes part of the liquid	46
distilled (water)	water that has been boiled and the steam has condensed to give pure water	78
drag	another name for air resistance	72
energy	when something has energy, it can make things move and cause things to change; all living things need energy to exist	24,66
environment	our natural surroundings	30

Acknowledgements

The authors and publisher are grateful for the permissions granted to reproduce copyright materials. While every effort has been made, it has not always been possible to identify the sources of all the materials used, or to trace all the copyright holders. If any omissions are brought to our notice, we will be happy to include the appropriate acknowledgements on reprinting.

The publisher is grateful to the experienced teachers Mansoora Shoaib Shah, Lahore Grammar School, 55 Main, Gulberg, Lahore and Lynne Ransford for their careful reviewing of the content.

p. 7 Alexander Semenov/ Science Photo Library; p. 10 Lucian Coman/ Shutterstock; p. 14 bikeriderlondon/ Shutterstock; p. 16 Stuart Monk/ Shutterstock; p. 17 Picsfive/ Shutterstock; p. 19 Gemenacom/ Shutterstock; p. 22 Malcolm Schuyl/ Alamy; p. 24 Ralph Loesche/ Shutterstock; p. 26tr Travel USA/ Alamy; p. 26bl Cathy Keifer/ Shutterstock; p. 26br Mike Raabe/Design Pics Inc./ Alamy; p. 27 nico99/ Shutterstock; p. 29 digitalunderwater.com/ Alamy; p. 30 Sue Cunningham/Worldwide Picture Library/ Alamy; p. 32t ssuaphotos/ Shutterstock; p. 32b John McKenna/ Alamy; p. 34 Vanessa Miles/ Alamy; p. 35t Rolf Bender/ Frank Lane Picture Agency; p. 35c Carolina Biological Supply Company/ Phototake/ Alamy; p. 35b Imagebroker/ Frank Lane Picture Agency; p. 36 Tony Wharton/ Frank Lane Picture Agency; p. 38 Kuzma/ Shutterstock; p. 38 Rebecca Hosking/ Frank Lane Picture Agency; p. 42 Bochkarev Photography/ Shutterstock; p. 43tr pogonici/ Shutterstock; p. 43tl Abel Tumik/ Shutterstock; p. 43b i love images/ Alamy; p. 45 Twin Design/ Shutterstock; p. 46 Elisabeth Coelfen/ Alamy; p. 47 GIPhotoStock/ Science Photo Library; p. 48 cvalle/ Shutterstock; p. 49 Gallo Images/ Alamy; p. 50 Iakov Filimonov/ Shutterstock; p. 51t Helene Rogers – Commercial/Art Directors & TRIP/ Alamy; p. 51b Robyn Mackenzie/ Shutterstock; p. 55 Jason Patrick Ross/ Shutterstock; p. 56 Robyn Mackenzie/ Shutterstock; p. 58 and p. 59t Martin F. Chillmaid/ Science Photo Library; p. 59b Dennis Hallinan/ Alamy; p. 60 Todd Warnock/Digital Vision/ Getty Images; p. 61 Rolf Richardson/age fotostock/ Alamy; p. 63 Fuse/ Getty Images; p. 65 Horizon International Images Limited/ Alamy; p. 66 Chris Cooper-Smith/ Alamy; p. 68l Rafa Irusta/ Shutterstock; p. 68r Elnur/ Shutterstock; p. 69 Thomas Müller/imagebroker/ Alamy; p. 71 Petar Ivanov Ishmiriev/ Shutterstock; p. 72 Richard Thornton/ Shutterstock; p. 73 Tom Tschida/ NASA; p. 74 Jack Sullivan/ Alamy; p. 78b stockyimages/ Shutterstock; p. 78c majeczka/ Shutterstock; p. 78t Tabby Mittins/ Shutterstock; p. 80 Bragin Alexey/ Shutterstock; p. 83 worldpix/ Alamy; p. 86 © Cynthia Classen/Flickr Open/ Getty Images; p. 88l sciencephotos/ Alamy; p. 88cl ekipaj/ iStockphoto; p. 88cr Krys Bailey/ Alamy; p. 88r David J. Green – engineering themes/ Alamy; p. 91 Christopher Brignell/ Thinkstock; p. 92t Bowl, Iran, Sasanian period, 4th-5th century (silver and gilt), Persian School/ Freer Gallery of Art, Smithsonian Institution, USA/ The Bridgeman Art Library; p. 92b Mary Evans Picture Library/ Alamy; p. 93 Sheila Terry/ Science Photo Library

Cover artwork: Bill Bolton

l = left, r = right, t = top, b = bottom, c = centre